D0918734

BOXING CHAMPIONS

OF THE HEAVYWEIGHT DIVISION
1882 - 2010

BOXING CHAMPIONS

OF THE HEAVYWEIGHT DIVISION
1 8 8 2 - 2 0 1 0

RONALD J. CURTIS

A BRIEF HISTORY OF THE GREAT CHAMPIONS FROM JOHN L. SULLIVAN
TO WLADIMIR KLITSCHKO WITH LOTS OF ACTION PICTURES

To order additional copies of this book, contact:
Xlibris Corporation
1-888-795-4274
www.Xlibris.com
Orders@Xlibris.com
71343

Contents

Promoters of the Century

Author's Note

The Boxing Champions of the Heavyweight Division is a work of nonfiction. It is about the fighters who became world heavyweight champions under the Queensberry rules. It includes information from the first world champion, John L. Sullivan, who was champion from 1882 through 1892, to the present-day champion. Included is a history of the early boxing game before Sullivan and the records that these heavyweight champions from Sullivan had set forth over a hundred years.

Prologue

I have always been interested in sports. As a child of fourteen in 1967, boxing and wrestling were my favorites to watch on television. I remember being so entranced with watching these sports that I soon began to collect related magazines and other literary pieces.

I can recall growing up on the farm meant that there were always chores to be done, for which I was paid meager earnings. With me being a child in the '60s and living on a secluded farm, my worries weren't focused on my mere earnings but how I was going to get to the store and spend my fifty cents on a boxing magazine. My father would always tell me to stop spending my money on those boxing magazines and save it for a rainy day, but his words never penetrated. I would buy the magazine anyway.

My focus was on obtaining as much knowledge as possible about the sports that I loved. Ever since those days on the farm, I have been researching, collecting, organizing, and constructing what lies before you. I hope that you will have as much joy reading this book as I had creating it. I present to you my ode to the great heavyweight boxing champions.

Writer's Comments

In writing this book on the heavyweight boxing champions, you will see names of so-called champions not in the book at all. This is because, in my opinion, they were not the actual champions in the first place.

As boxing fans read this book, they will see that there are titles vacant for different reasons. In 1905 when the title was vacant, Marvin Hart was a so-called champion who would not be in this book. Hart and Jack Root were handpicked by the retired champion, Jim Jeffries, to fight for the title. Better fighters were out there.

Hart and Root were unimpressive fighters. Hart won the fight. Because Jim Jeffries wasn't qualified and had picked two unimpressive, mediocre fighters, many references on boxing do not list Hart as champion. They do all believe that when Tommy Burns beat Hart in 1906, we had a true champion.

Some sixty years after Marvin Hart, Jimmy Ellis would be considered as champion by another title vacancy. Ellis is also not in this book as champion because he was said to be champion, as also Joe Frazier was, at this time with the stripping of Muhammad Ali's title. This was settled with Frazier and Ellis fighting each other and Frazier winning and becoming the real champion.

Another fighter, Ernie Terrell, was called champion in 1965. To me, this isn't right because Muhammad Ali gave Sonny Liston a rematch after winning the title. Terrell isn't champion because he didn't beat Ali in the ring. Ali would settle everything when he fought and beat Terrell in 1967.

Like Ernie Terrell, Ken Norton was named champion. Leon Spinks, the champion, gave Ali a rematch after winning the title and didn't fight Norton.

An even worse example of so-called world heavyweight champion is the period when Larry Holmes was world champion from 1978 to 1985. In his almost eight years as champion, there were eight so-called champions. They were John Tate, Mike Weaver, Michael Dokes, Gerrie Coetzee, Tim Witherspoon, Pinklon Thomas, Greg Page, and Tony Tubbs. All of these guys were said to be world champions even though Larry Holmes was still an undefeated world champion.

This does not make any sense at all. In this book, I have only the undisputed champions, the lineal champion, or the *Ring Magazine* champion. They mostly believe that to be the champion, you had to beat the champion; and if there was a retirement involved, the top two or top three fighters would fight for the undisputed heavyweight championship.

The situation would get worse in the 1990s and 2000s when the sanctioning bodies would have multiple champions at the same time for years. When you, as a reader, get to the 1990s and 2000s, you will see all the names, what titles they held, and why I do not consider them as world heavyweight champions. I pick up again the real champion who I figure is the true champion.

Acknowledgments

These boxing champions are entertainers. Their stage is the boxing ring.

There are so many people to give thanks to past and present, especially the first-rate reportage of daily and old sports journalists in magazines, books, and the daily newspaper. Without them, a work of this magnitude could not have been accomplished.

This piece has many inspirations including *Black Champion, Boxing Illustrated, Boxing Illustration, Boxing and Wrestling, Guinness Boxing, History of Boxing, International Boxing, The Encyclopedia of Boxing, The Illustrated Home Library Encyclopedia, The Ring, World Book Encyclopedia, World Boxing*, and computers.

Lastly, gratefully appreciated is the considerable amount of help executed by Myra Burley, Tamika Harris, Valeria LaSane, Joan Middleton, Anika Curtis, Linda Curtis, and Dorka Woodard. This piece would not have been completed without their contributions.

I would like to give a special thanks to Terry Woodard who, like myself, is a Sherwin-Williams employee. I have been writing this book, as a hobby, for over forty years. Terry was the only person that I allowed to take my material home to read it. Terry not only liked what I had compiled but also encouraged me to have it published. Of all of the publishing companies that I had investigated, I decided to choose Xlibris Publishers, which was the one that Terry had suggested. He has always given me good advice, and I consider him as a true friend.

Introduction

Ancient Times

Boxing is one of the oldest known sports. Records have been found that indicate the ancient Sumerians practiced the sport at least five thousand years ago in what is now Iraq. In ancient Rome and Greece over two thousand years ago, boxing was such a brutal sport that the fighters usually continued until one or the other was dead. Boxing was and still is a brutal sport, but many people like it.

Prizefighters

Prizefights started in England over two hundred years ago. Money was put into a purse, or prize, and then two fighters would compete for it. These boxers were known as prizefighters.

The Revival of Boxing

Boxing almost disappeared as a sport until the 1700s when it was revived in England. Historians credit James Figg (1695-1734) with originating bare-knuckle or gloveless fighting. With the help of James Figg, who defeated every fighter to be champion of England, the interest in the game became very popular and grew. Because of James Figg, by 1719 the fight game was big again, and he was the first champion. Figg retired from the ring.

He later retired and opened the first gymnasium for boxers, known as Figgs Academy for Boxing. Soon boxing began to be very popular and spread from England to America.

During Figg's years the fight game was not all boxing. It was gloveless fighting. You could use your hands to wrestle a person down and a lot of other things that did not involve boxing. Figg believed that men should fight until one of them had obviously won, no matter what. Figg's method did not provide rest periods for a specified time. Figg was inducted into the Ring Boxing Hall of Fame in 1954 and the International Boxing Hall of Fame in 1992.

James Figg

Rules

As the sport of boxing became more and more popular, there soon came the need to have rules. In 1743 the fighter Jack Broughton (1704-1789), who became the English champion, set up a set of rules for boxing. He is known as the father of boxing. His rules help change the wrestling type of fighting, the kicking, eye gouging, and only having a fighter second in the fight area. Before this rule was set, there could be different people around the fight area, and they could be somewhat involved in the fight. He also set the rule that you could not strike an opponent when he was down on his knees or below the waist or seize him by the hair; he also set umpires to settle disputes about the battle. Almost everything else went on. The rules that Broughton set in 1743 lasted until 1838 when the Broughton's rules change to the London Prize Ring rules. These were additional rules that were already there to become standard. Seconds could not be in the ring, except between rounds — everything to make the boxing game safer and lessen the brutality of prizefighting in England. Broughton was inducted into the Ring Boxing Hall of Fame in 1954 and the International Boxing Hall of Fame in 1990.

Jack Broughton

English Fighters

Through the 1700s the Englishmen were what you would call the real good fighters. Fighters from all over the world would come to England to fight and hope to get a name.

American Fighters

Most of the American fighters appeared in Britain and England. The first American to make a name for himself was a former slave named Bill Richmond (1763-1829), who won his freedom by fighting. From 1791 to 1818 at the age of fifty-five, he was a top and popular fighter in London, England. In doing so he was the first man born in America to win high honors in the ring. Richmond was inducted into the International Boxing Hall of Fame in 1999.

Bill Richmond

Boxing in the United States

Fighting in America came late because the ones that could fight went overseas to fight. England had their first champion in James Figg in 1719. United States didn't have their first champion until 1841, when Tom Hyer beat Country McClusky.

Boxing in the United States met widespread opposition during its early days. It was illegal in most areas, and the police often broke up prizefights. Bouts drew small crowds that watched boxers battle with bare knuckles. John L. Sullivan was given the chief credit for popularizing boxing. Sullivan noticed that police tolerated matches held under the Queensberry rules. The Sullivan fights became famous and made the sport popular throughout the country.

New York legalized boxing in 1896 but repealed the law in 1900. A later law permitted boxing in private clubs. But it also was repealed; in 1920, New York passed the Walker law, which permitted public prizefights. Within a few years, other states legalized boxing and established commissions to regulate the sport.

Bare Knuckles

Over one hundred fifty years after James Figg, the fights were with bare knuckles and were fights to the finish. You could only win by a knockout or one of the fighters gave up. A round only ended when a person was knocked down. Bare-knuckle fighting was illegal but still went on. Many times the fighters were arrested, and the spectators were sent home.

Queensberry Rules: From Bare Knuckles to Gloves

Until the late 1800s, boxers fought with bare knuckles under the London Prize Ring rules. In 1867 a British sportsman, the Marquis of Queensberry, sponsored the establishment of a new set of boxing rules. The major improvement was to wear boxing gloves. The wearing of gloves is a safety factor in the protection of the boxer's hands, like getting a broken finger or hand that would keep a fighter out of the ring longer than normal. Other rules that came under the Queensberry rules were having three-minute rounds, a one-minute rest period, and a ten-second count for a knockout. These rules, with some modification, still govern amateur and professional boxing. The Queensberry rules were not followed completely in a fight until 1872, when the first match with gloves was held in London. The last bare-knuckle championship fight took place in 1889, when John L. Sullivan defeated Jake Kilrain in Richburg, Mississippi. Historians generally credit James J. Corbett with being the first boxer to win a championship under the Queensberry rules. He defeated Sullivan in New Orleans in 1892.

First World Champion

The John L. Sullivan and Jake Kilrain was the last bare-knuckle fight. Sullivan was considered the first world champion because he was the champion at the time boxing adopted the Queensberry rules. Sullivan won the title fighting bare-knuckle, but when he lost it to James Corbett in 1892, he was wearing gloves.

The Sanctioning Bodies of the Heavyweight Division

By Ronald Curtis

The sanctioning bodies are the governing organizations which make the rules; have complete authority to rule, to run without having any other organization over them, to have their own champion; have their own top contenders to the title, and have the legal authority and the obligation.

There are many sanctioning bodies; these are the top four that really run boxing:

1. (WBA) World Boxing Association, which started in 1921 as the (NBC National Boxing Council, and change to the WBA in 1963
2. (WBC) World Boxing Council, which started in 1963
3. (IBF) International Boxing Federation, which started in 1983
4. (WBO) World Boxing Organization, which started in 1988

Before the 1980s everybody knew who the world champion was. You didn't have all these sanctioning bodies. If there was a confusion of who was the champion, it would be settled right away with a fight for the undisputed championship of the world. In 1967 Muhammad Ali was the world champion, and Ernie Terrell was the WBA champion because Ali joined the Nation of Islam. Ali won and unified the heavyweight division. In 1968 you had two champions: Joe Frazier, the New York Boxing Commission and five states' champion; and Jimmy Ellis, the WBA champion. Frazier and Ellis would fight in 1970, with Frazier winning to unify the heavyweight division.

The Sanctioning Bodies: Problems I Had with It

The top four sanctioning bodies are the WBC, WBA, IBF, and the WBO. All four of them are big and have power in what's going on in boxing. Some may recognize the same fighter as champion; half of them may have a different champion, or all could have a different champion at the same time.

All four sanctioning bodies have the power to have their own top ranking of fighters and the power to strip a champion of his title. It can happen that while one sanctioning body may have a man as champion, the other sanctions may not even have him rated as a top ten contender if the two sanctioning are feuding with each other; and if some of the sanctioning bodies agree on a champion and if that champion did not fight their top contender, they could strip the champion of the title. By that sanctioning having a new champion, the other sanctioning still have the other champion to be beaten; this is a problem because you could have a lot of number one contenders and a lot of so-called world champions, or have a vacant champion in that sanctioning at the same time. You could lose a real good champion, not even beaten in the ring, for a champion who is not as good, with the different sanctioning bodies; even the champions got involved by giving up one of the smaller sanctioning belt for the bigger sanction belt.

This was difficult for me in writing this book. I started writing this book in 1967, and I stopped in the middle 1990s. I stopped because of the number of different champions at the same time for years. There was no undisputed champion from 1992 until 1999, and the sanctioning bodies were not trying hard enough to unify the title. I stopped after George Foreman was stripped of the title in 1995.1 am going to give you a list of champions or so-called champions from 1996 through 1998.

(1996)

Michael Moorer, IBF
Mike Tyson, WBC
Evander Holyfield, WBA
Bruce Seldon, WBA

Frank Bruno, WBC
Oliver McCall, WBC
Riddick Bowe, WBO
Henry Akinwande, WBO

(1997)

Michael Moorer, IBF
Lennox Lewis, WBC
Oliver McCall, WBC
Henry Akinwande, WBO
Herbie Hide, WBO
Evander Holyfield, IBF and WBA

(1998)

Herbie Hide, WBO
Evander Holyfield, WBA and IBF
Lennox Lewis, WBC

With a list of multiple champions like this from 1996 to 1998, I had to stop writing. To get enough information on this many a champion, with a lot of them champions at the same time, is too hard to do; plus I wouldn't be writing about the true champion most of the time. In the '60s, '70s, and the '80s, I could write because I knew who the champion was. Then in the '90s, I had to stop because there were a lot of champions, hardly any undisputed champion or a unification of title.

A Plan to Write Again

I got back into writing this book, learning about two organizations, the Lineal Champion and the *Ring Magazine* non-sanctioning bodies; both organizations are pretty much the same. The Lineal Champion says that the one who beats the champion, who beat the champion, is the champion. You have to beat the reigning champion, the real champion in the ring. If there are no champions at the time, then the top two fighters fight for the undisputed championship.

The *Ring Magazine* is a boxing magazine. The way to become the champion is to beat the true reigning or, if there are no champions at the time, to have a fight between the number one and the number two contender. There are only three ways of losing the ring title: lose a championship fight, move to a different weight class, or retire. Boxing fans today say that the best ranking of top fighters is not that of the sanctioning bodies but the ranking made by the *Ring Magazine*.

I believe in what the Lineal Champion and the *Ring Magazine* believe in. The two words are undisputed" and unified. Undisputed means that there is only one champion. Unified means that if there are no champions or if there are two champions, they will have a championship fight to unify the belts.

Starting with George Foreman, 1995

George Foreman won the title in 1994. In 1995 he won a controversial decision over Axel Sculz that everybody thought Sculz had won. Foreman refused to give an order rematch to Axel Schulz. He would go on and fight easier fights. He never fought the top fighters Lennox Lewis, Mike Tyson, Evander Holyfield, or Axel Sculz. Foreman was stripped of his title in 1995. To me, by Foreman not wanting to fight the number one contender, just trying to hold the title, the sanctioning bodies were correct in rightfully stripping Foreman of his title.

The stripping of Foreman of his title would open the door for all the champions. You would have from 1996 through 1999 Foreman, the champion who beat Michael Moorer for the title in 1994, who beat the 1992 undisputed champion Evander Holyfield who beat the 1992 undisputed champion Riddick Bowe who beat the 1992 undisputed champion Evander Holyfield who beat the 1990 undisputed champion Buster Douglas who beat the 1989 undisputed champion Mike Tyson.

Starting With Lennox Lewis, 1999

I go by the Lineal Champion and the *Ring Magazine* which both say to have an undisputed world heavyweight champion.

By saying this, I will start writing about the champions with Lennox Lewis, who beat Evander Holyfield for the undisputed world champion in November of 1999. From 1996 up till Lewis unified the belts, I will just write the champion's name and what sanctioning bodies that they belonged to.

YEARS THEY WERE CHAMPIONS

John L. Sullivan	February 1882-September 1892
James J. Corbett	September 1892-March 1897
Robert Fitzsimmons	March 1897-June 1899
James Jefferies	June 1899-May 1905 (retired)
Title Vacant	
Tommy Burns	February 1906-December 1908
Jack Johnson	December 1908-April 1915
Jess Willard	April 1915-July 1919
Jack Dempsey	July 1919-September 1926
Gene Tunney	September 1926-August 1928 (retired)
Title Vacant	
Max Schmeling	June 1930-June 1932
Jack Sharkey	June 1932-June 1933
Primo Carnera	June 1933-June 1934
Max Baer	June 1934-June 1935
James Braddock	June 1935-June 1937
Joe Louis	June 1937-March 1949 (retired)
Title Vacant	
Ezzard Charles	June 1949-July 1951
Jersey Joe Walcott	July 1951-September 1952
Rocky Marciano	September 1952-April 1956 (retired)
Title Vacant	
Floyd Patterson	November 1956-June 1959
Ingemar Johansson	November 1959-June 1960
Floyd Patterson	June 1960-September 1962
Sonny Liston	September 1962-February 1964
Cassius Clay	February 1964-April 1968
(Muhammed Ali)	(stripped of title)
Title Vacant	
Joe Frazier	February 1970-January 1973

George Foreman	January 1973-October 1974
Muhammed Ali	February 1974-February 1978
Leon Spinks	February 1978-September 1978
Muhammed Ali	September 1978-October 1978 (retired)
Title Vacant	
Larry Holmes	June 1978-September 1985
Michael Spinks	September 1985-February 1987 (stripped of title)
Title Vacant	
Mike Tyson	August 1987-February 1990
James (Buster) Douglas	February 1990-October 1990
Evander Holyfield	October 1990-November 1992
Riddick Bowe	November 1992-November 1993
Evander Holyfield	November 1993-April 1994
Michael Moorer	April 1994-November 1994
George Foreman	November 1994-June 1995 (stripped of title)

Title Vacant as World Champion

In my opinion, after George Foreman beat the champion to be the champion, there was a big confusion regarding who was the world heavyweight champion. From 1996 to 1999, the sanctioning bodies had a big list of some undeserving champions that are called world heavyweight champions.

From 1996 to 1999, I do not list these champions like I do the other champions in the book. They never pitted the top two fighters together to have one champion like the *Ring Magazine* would do. There was no undisputed world champion. This would change in 1999 when Lennox Lewis was the undisputed world heavyweight champion. I will list the name and title that was held from 1996 to 1999.

(1996)

Michael Moorer, IBF; Mike Tyson, WBC
Evander Holyfield, WBA; Bruce Seldon, WBA
Frank Bruno, WBC; Oliver McCall, WBC
Riddick Bowe, WBO; Henry Akinwande, WBC

(1997)

Michael Moorer, IBF; Lennox Lewis, WBC
Oliver McCall, WBC; Henry Akinwande, WBO
Herbie Hide, WBO; Evander Holyfield, IBF and WBA

(1998)

Herbie Hide, WBO; Evander Holyfield, IBF and WBA
Lennox Lewis, WBC

YEARS THEY WERE CHAMPION

Lennox Lewis	November 1999-April 2001
Hasim Rahman	April 2001-November 2001
Lennox Lewis	November 2001-February 2004 (retired)
Vitali Klitschko	April 2004-November 2005 (retired)

Title Vacant as World Champion

(My Opinion) Like 1996 to 1999, boxing had the same problem with the retirement of Vitali Klitschko. From 2006 to 2009, there is another list of the sanctioning bodies world heavyweight champions—some undeserving—another confusion regarding who is the world heavyweight champion. The *Ring Magazine* would have the top two fighters fight in 2009, with Wladimir Klitschko winning to be the champion. I will again list the name and title that was held from 2006 to 2009.

(2006)

Lamon Brewster, WBO; Flasim Rahman, WBC
Sergei Liakhovich, WBO; Wladimir Klitschko, IBF
Oleg Maskaev, WBC; Shannon Briggs, WBO

(2007)

Wladimir Klitschko, IBF; Oleg Maskaev, WBC
Shannon Briggs, WBO; Rusian Chagaer, WBA
Sultan Ibrogimov, WBO

(2008)

Sultan Ibragimov, WBO; Wladimir Klitschko, IBF and WBO
Samuel Peter, WBC; Rusian Chagaev, WBA

YEARS THEY WERE CHAMPION

Wladimir Klitschko   June 2009-Present

John L. Sullivan

John L. Sullivan as he looked in his prime. Only five feet ten inches tall with a peak fighting weight of 190 pounds, he packed tremendous power in his right hand.

1889: John L. Sullivan (left) and Jack Kilrain in the last bare-knuckle championship fight, staged at Richburg, Mississippi.

John L. Sullivan

Born: 1858-1918; Boston, Massachusetts
Weight: 195 lbs., 5'10"
Champion: 1882-1892

Won: 38   Lost: 1   Drew: 3   Knockouts: 33

John L. Sullivan was the last bare-knuckle champion. His fistic rise began in 1878 at the age of nineteen. He would fight anywhere: in the ring, in a saloon, or in the streets.

Sullivan always fought as a slugger. Because he was the slugger, he was the boss in the ring. He possessed more knowledge of ring work than most men and especially more than the big fighters of his day. He was known to have tremendous power in his right hand. From the opening bell, Sullivan would rush out and overwhelm his opponent with awesome power and unexpected speed. At five feet ten and 195 pounds, he was a giant for his time. Sullivan was known as the Boston Strong Boy. None of his opponents had much chance of winning, and most were knocked out in one or two rounds.

At the age of sixteen, he was a good athletics boy, first baseball and later boxing. Even then Sullivan was referred to as Strong Boy; among his playmates as a fighter, he was invincible.

At a young age, Sullivan did odd jobs including playing and getting paid to play semipro baseball. While he was doing these odd jobs, he also had some amateur fights where it became known that he had a heavy punch.

In 1878 Sullivan fought a contender for the title named Johnny Woods. He got a quick knockout over Woods and started getting big attention in the boxing world. The next year he defeated Don Dwyer, the champion of Massachusetts, and was getting more fame.

It soon became apparent to Sullivan and his manager that he could win the title. They began to put up fifty dollars that no man could last four rounds with him, even the champion Paddy Ryan. They did this in every state they were in.

After winning nearly all his fights in early rounds, Sullivan got the chance to fight Paddy Ryan for the championship on February 7, 1882. The match was no match, for Sullivan was too strong and hit too hard for Ryan to do anything as Sullivan applied pressure in every round, leading up to knocking out Ryan in the ninth round for the title at the age of twenty-three.

Even though Paddy Ryan was the champion before him, Sullivan was considered the first world champion because he was the first champion to fight with gloves under the Queensberry rules.

After winning the title, Sullivan was a busy fighter. He loved to fight and figured no man on earth could beat him, as he continued to win on early round knockouts. From 1884 to 1886, he had fourteen wins, fighting any challengers.

Sullivan went on a nine-month sparring tour of the United States after winning the title in 1882. On this tour his manager offered one thousand dollars to any man who stayed four rounds with Sullivan. About fifty men tried to win the reward but failed, all being knocked out in a few minutes.

In one of the oddest matches in heavyweight history, Sullivan fought a challenger name G. M. Robinson on March 6, 1884. In this match Sullivan won an easy victory, with Robinson going down sixty-eight times to avoid punishment.

Before he became champion and while he was champion, he fought mostly as a bare-knuckle fighter.

Out of all the heavyweight champions, Sullivan was the only champion who was allowed to gamble outside of the boxing ring. He would bet money that no man could beat him or go four rounds with him, gaining a lot of fame going on tour, putting up one thousand dollars.

He was known as the Boston Strong Boy, and the world loved him. John always enjoyed himself as being the champion and let people know it. He always liked to let the world know that he could lick anybody, and he would prove it in or out of the ring.

Sullivan's championship rule was marred by reckless lifestyle that put him on a collision course with disaster. He was a very loud man who had an outrageous temper. He loved to go to saloons and brag that he could whip anybody in the house, while buying drinks for everybody. He paid a fortune in courts for petty fines. Police competed with each other to arrest him. The champion liked to go on prolonged drinking binges. He also liked to eat, and between title defenses, his weight ballooned to more than 230 pounds.

On July 7, 1889, Sullivan fought Jake Kilrain for the title. In a hard-fought fight, he beat Kilrain in the seventy-fifth round. This would be the last title fight fought under the London Prize Ring rules where bare knuckles were used. After this fight, gloves were mandatory.

After winning his fight with Jake Kilrain, Sullivan would be out of the ring for over three years, except for fighting exhibitions. All this time by not fighting, he was not taking good care of his body to stay in shape. During those three years, he was getting older and also was drinking very hard. The young fighters knew this too, and they wanted to fight him for the title.

Sullivan knew about the young fighters who wanted to fight him, saying that he would fight any man who put up an outside bet of ten thousand dollars.

Jim Corbett would be the young fighter who would put up the money for the title fight with Sullivan. Going into the fight, Sullivan still believed he could lick any man in the world and took Corbett lightly. He trained lightly and continued to drink. By not training right, Sullivan came into the fight over 20 pounds overweight, weighing in at 212 pounds. This would be the first heavyweight championship fight to be fought with gloves on under the Marquis of Queensbury rules.

The fight between Sullivan and Corbett took place on September 6, 1892. In the fight Sullivan was too slow, overweight, and too old as he stumbled and staggered around the ring. For this fight, Corbett was in great shape weighing in at 178 pound and too young, too agile, and too skillful for Sullivan. He took away Sullivan's power; he danced and dogged away from Sullivan's attacks. By the twenty-first round, Sullivan was a tired, beaten fighter, and got counted out. After losing his title to Corbett,

Sullivan would say, "I can only say that I am glad that I had been beaten by an American." The whole world was in shock after he lost his title to Corbett. He had been a hero to all boxing fans throughout the world for the ten long years he was champion.

After his boxing career, he had some hard years as he continued to drink hard and get drunk. Sometime barely getting by with the money, he changed his way of living by finally quitting drinking in 1905. He would appear on stage and gave lectures on not to drink, always drawing big crowds. Everybody wanted to see the great John L. Sullivan.

During his ten years as champion, he fought all around the world. The only bad thing on his record was a thirty-nine-round draw with Charlie Mitchell in March of 1888; Sullivan wanted to beat Mitchell real bad because he was the English champion; knocking Mitchell down fifteen times, he still did not really beat Mitchell. With the draw with Mitchell, Sullivan was still considered as the world champion.

Sullivan would never risk his title in a match with a black fighter. At the time there was a black fighter named Peter Jackson, who was one of the great heavyweight fighters of all time, who is also in World Boxing Hall of Fame as a member of pioneer groups; Sullivan would not fight him because he had already drawn the color line. He said, "It is not right for a white man to fight a black man."

When Sullivan was champion, he was a very proud man, in and out of the ring in a lot of different ways. He knew that he could lick any man in the world. He would let everybody know this by his bragging that he could, against fighters and non-fighters. He would fight in the ring, in bars, and in the streets. With his outrageous temper, his boldness would always come out.

The name John L. Sullivan was his name, and he loved it, and he let everybody around him at the time know his name was John L. Sullivan. Whatever he was talking about, he would end it with "Yours truly, John L. Sullivan" or with "John L. Sullivan himself."

When it came to drinking, he loved it, letting people know how much a big amount he could handle, which was always a big amount. He would say he could drink more than anyone in the house.

Sullivan had forty-two professional fights, losing just once. He scored thirty-three knockouts with fourteen first-round knockouts. He lost his title after ten years to James Corbett in the twenty-first round. At that time he was thirty-three years old, past his prime and a fat 212 pounds.

All boxers owed something to Sullivan for this tremendous personality and gift for publicity. Both naturally and by design, Sullivan made such good newspaper copy that he had bought professional boxing from the barge, the back room, from "not knowing you would be arrested for fighting" or "getting paid for the fight," and the private athletic club into public where tickets could be sold out and fortunes could be made. His tours around the country made him the first American to be popular not only in America but also in foreign countries. The first American athlete of any kind to be a national sports idol, champions after Sullivan would also fight in foreign countries and gain fame.

It is safe to say that modern era of boxing began on February 7, 1882, when the great John L. Sullivan knocked out Paddy Ryan and won the heavyweight championship and five thousand dollars.

As he continued on stage and giving lectures and drawing big crowds, he died in 1918. Before he died in 1918, he had quit one of his biggest problems for thirteen years, drinking.

James (Jim) Corbett

Sullivan always avoided fighting Jackson, but Corbett agreed to meet him, and they fought sixty-one rounds to a draw. Ringside drawing of the Jim Corbett-Peter Jackson classic at San Francisco, May 21, 1890.

James J. Corbett, a former San Francisco bank clerk, introduced science to boxing. He was the first fighter to employ the left jab as an effective offensive weapon.

Gentleman Jim Corbett was the first modern-day heavyweight champion and one of the first pure boxers. He won the title in 1892 and lost it to Fitzsimmons in 1897.

The first heavyweight fight under the Queensbury rules 1892: Sullivan and James J. Corbett in their championship match in New Orleans. Corbett won by a knockout in the twenty-first round.

James "Jim" Corbett

Born: 1866-1933
Weight: 180 lbs., 6'1"
Champion: 1892-1897

Won: 11   Lost: 4   Drew: 2   Knockouts: 7

James Corbett was the first modern-day champion because he won the title under the Queensberry rules using gloves. He also was the first scientific boxer and the first to use the left jab as an effective weapon. The fighters before him were toe-to-toe, flat-footed fighters. When talking about Corbett, you are talking about the father of scientific boxing.

As a fighter he was quick, a hard hitter, and very smart for his time. He not only had public-school education in San Francisco but was also educated at Catholic College of the Sacred Heart.

Living in San Francisco, Corbett was a bank clerk and a fighter. Being in a family with a lot of brothers, they built a sort of ring, and they would box each other; when not fighting his brothers, he would have other regular fights in town.

While still working as a bank teller, he joined the San Francisco Olympic Club when he was eighteen years old. At the club he joined the boxing team there. Fighting at the club is where he really learned to fight. He soon became the champion at the club. Fighting fans soon learned that Corbett was very quick of hand and foot and very hard to hit by the slow fighters of his era.

At the age of eighteen, Corbett had his first professional fight in 1884. His opponent was Dave Eisemanny whom he beat in two rounds.

When he defeated Joe Choynski, a good fighter, he was on his way. They nicknamed him Gentleman Jim because he dressed well, had good looks, manners, and taste. He also had his successful stage acting.

On February 18, 1890, Corbett fought Jake Kilrain. Kilrain was considered the second best fighter in the world, only the great John L. Sullivan was ranked ahead of him. In the fight with Kilrain, Corbett beat Kilrain in nine rounds.

Kilrain had gone seventy-five tough rounds with champion John L. Sullivan. With this win over Kilrain, it made Corbett a top contender.

Then he signed to fight Peter Jackson. This was one of Corbett's most historic fights. This is the same top black contender to have a shot at John L. Sullivan's title whom Sullivan always avoided on account of his being a black fighter.

Unlike Sullivan, Corbett agreed to meet Jackson on May 21, 1890. At the time Corbett was a young and upcoming fighter. It was youth vs. age, even though Corbett was conceding thirty-six pounds. They fought sixty-one rounds; both men were physically unable to continue the fight, and the referee decided it was a draw. Corbett was a polished fighter and a superb ring strategist. With the win over Kilrain and the draw with Jackson, two top contenders, Corbett was in line to fight Sullivan for the title. Even though Jim was now a top contender, it did not mean anything to the boxing public because everybody figured that no man could beat the champion John L. Sullivan. Only Corbett knew he could beat Sullivan when he got the chance.

Jim got his chance in 1892 to fight Sullivan for the title. He knew he could beat Sullivan by making him miss with speed and using scientific skills. In the first heavyweight fight under the Queensberry rules, Corbett was much too young at twenty-six. His scientific approach, which he used against Sullivan with his hand and foot speed, was too much for the flat-footed Sullivan.

From the start of the fight, Corbett stayed away from the power of Sullivan. As the fight went on, Corbett began to carry the fight. Sullivan was being beaten to the punch as he tried to attack, only to be bewildered by the young Corbett. His constant moving around the ring wore Sullivan out, winning the championship in the twenty-first round.

After Corbett defeated Sullivan, it became apparent for the first time that science could overcome brute strength and slugging ability, provided it was backed with a punch, enough to put the other man out. After winning the championship from Sullivan, it took a while for the boxing fans to give in to Corbett. They could not get over Sullivan, their hero, losing the title to Corbett. With his scientific skill in the ring and his gentleman-like behavior, he earned the respect of the boxing fans.

A year and a half went by before he made a defense of his title. His first defense was against Charlie Mitchell, the champion of England on January 25, 1894. This was the same Mitchell who had fought to a draw with John L. Sullivan.

In the Mitchell fight, Corbett appeared to have lost the first round. By the second round, Corbett was in control as he knocked Mitchell down. The third round was no match as Corbett fought a relentless fight, landing blow after blow to Mitchell. He sent Mitchell down, who managed to get up, only to be sent down the final time for the win. With Corbett beating Mitchell, the champion from England, it gave the United States its first undisputed world champion.

It was during Corbett's reign as champion that the shift of fighters started coming to the United States from all over the world. Not only the world champion was in the States, but the money was here.

Corbett's next defense of his title was against Bob Fitzsimmons on March 17, 1897. In the fight against Fitzsimmons, Corbett was doing well in the early rounds, winning them fairly easy. In the sixth round, he knocked Fitzsimmons down and bloodied him. As the fight went longer, Corbett began to tire. He lost the fight and his title in the fourteenth round when Fitzsimmons hit him with a solid left hook to the pit of his stomach. His breath was knocked out of him. As he was gasping for air, he was counted out. It was a big upset. The nation figured Corbett was far superior.

Two years after losing this title, Corbett wanted his title back. He signed to fight the current champion Jim Jeffries. In the fight against Jeffries, Corbett fought a great fight handling Jeffries for twenty rounds with his scientific style and speed, having his way for most of the fight with a lot of punches unanswered. As the fight went on, piling up enough points to win the title, Corbett began to tire. His legs were gone, and his age began to show. Jim got trapped on the ropes and fell prey to the powerful Jeffries in the twenty-third round.

Three years later on August 4, 1903, Jim made a final comeback to win the title. His third comeback wasn't as good as his second comeback against Jim Jeffries. This time at the age of thirty-seven, he was knocked out by Jeffries in the tenth round. This was Corbett's last fight. After his second loss to Jeffries, he played in the theater and died in 1933 at the age of sixty-seven.

This was an era in which winners were rewarded with a huge share of the purse, while the losers received only a portion. The winner of the fight was to be rewarded with nine thousand dollars, the loser with five hundred dollars.

Robert "Fitz" Fitzsimmons

One of the earliest fight photographs: Corbett deflects Fitzsimmons's right in the eleventh round.

Ruby Robert Fitzsimmons, who won the title from Jim Corbett in 1897, was the most devastating fighter in early heavyweight history. He lost his title in 1899.

A clinch before Fitzsimmons delivered his "solar plexus" punch in the fourteenth round to end the fight.

One of boxing's early "tater men" was the "Fighting Blacksmith" Bob Fitzsimmons, who won the heavyweight title with a one-punch knockout over Jim Corbett.

Robert "Bob" Fitzsimmons

Born: 1863-1917, England
Weight: 172 lbs., 6'
Champion: 1897-1899

Won: 43   Lost: 12   Drew: 0   Knockouts: 32

Bob Fitzsimmons was the middleweight who took on and beat the finest heavyweight of this time.

As a fighter he was known as Fitz or Bob. A very devastating hitter, some of his early opponents were knocked unconscious by blows that landed on points not considered winnable: to the forehead, ear, and chest. Fitz's hitting power came from helping his father in a blacksmith shop.

By being born in England, he was the only heavyweight champion from England. He left England at an early age and grew up in New Zealand. Growing up in New Zealand, he only wanted to be a blacksmith. He began to become known as a good fighter.

Fitzsimmons first appearance in the ring was at Jem Mace amateur boxing tournament in New Zealand in 1883. Jem Mace, the champion at the time, was touring New Zealand for a boxing tournament. Fitz decided to enter it.

Fitzsimmons, being the small fighter that he was, weighed only 140 pounds at the time. He was warned by the champion Mace about being too small to be opposing heavyweight, but he entered anyway. Although small in size when counting weight, he had strong arms, back muscles, and could hit very hard. Fitz went on to knock out four men to win the amateur championship of New Zealand, and that began thirty years in boxing.

The very next year, Jem Mace gave another tournament. This time Fitzsimmons knocked out five men in a night to win the tournament.

At the beginning Fitzsimmons fought mostly as a middleweight under the London rules, which consisted of bare fists; with his size being small, the London rules, which allows some wrestling, was not to his advantage but to a bigger fighter. This didn't stop Fitzsimmons as he continued to knock out his opponents.

Fitzsimmons soon left New Zealand and went to Australia. At this time he was weighing about 148 pounds and was knocking out middleweights and heavyweights. After having a good reputation and knocking fighters out in Australia, he sailed to fight in America. In 1891 Fitzsimmons moved to California to fight mostly as a middleweight. His first two fights in America was knockout victory. After winning all his fights in the state, he signed to fight the middleweight champion, the original Jack Dempsey, on January 14, 1891. The fight with Dempsey was all Fitzsimmons as he gave Dempsey a sound beating throughout the fight, landing many solid punches. After Dempsey was knocked down the sixth, tenth, eleventh, and twelfth rounds, his cornerman threw in the towel, making Fitzsimmons the new middleweight champion of the world who began to gain fame.

A very serious tragedy would put Fitzsimmons in the ring on November 19, 1894, that affected Fitzsimmons in wanting to continue to fight or how he would fight from then on. In a four-round exhibition fight with Con Riordan, Fitzsimmons hit Riordan with a hard right to the head and a hard left to the heart. Riordan went down and could not get up; Con Riordan was dead. Con Riordan's death affected Fitzsimmons a lot; he didn't want to fight again. Having killed a fighter in the ring, he was talked to about coming back to the ring. He was told that he had done too well to quit now. He changed his mind and came back to continue what was a great boxing career.

Coming back to the ring, Fitzsimmons wasn't the same fighter at first as he was. In fights he was holding back his punches, didn't really want to go real hard with the punches. He kept thinking of the Riordan fight. He had to be told over and over that what happened in the Riordan fight wasn't his fault for his death was an accident.

After beating all the middleweights, Fitzsimmons began to think about the heavyweights. His last fight as a middleweight was in 1895. He won on a knockout over Dan Creedon. By 1896

Fitzsimmons was fighting as a heavyweight. He had good success fighting the top contenders in the heavyweight division, even though he weighed about 172 pounds. He was winning most of his fights by hitting the fighters in the body, while most fighters were winning their fights by going to the head. His best punch was a punch to the stomach, which will go on to be called "the solar plexus punch." At this time in his career, he was the best body puncher in the game.

Solar plexus punch is a punch located toward the pit of the stomach with a right or left uppercut delivered to the soft spot of the body. With this punch, he won many fights.

Before coming to the United States, Fitzsimmons had a four-round loss to Jem Hall before getting a chance at the title; he got a rematch with Hall in the States and knocked out Hall in four rounds. Then he had a win over Joe Choyski, a top contender to the title.

Having success fighting heavyweights, including a twelve-round knockout over Peter Maher, the Irish heavyweight champion, Fitz wanted the heavyweight title held by Jim Corbett. Corbett agreed to fight Fitzsimmons on March 17, 1897. Fitz weighed only 167 pounds for this fight. During the fight Corbett was winning most of the fight, round by round. After the sixth round, things began to change in Fitzsimmons's favor as he started to work on Corbett's body in slowing him down. In the fourteenth round, Fitz threw a left solar plexus punch to Corbett's stomach with so much force that he couldn't get up for the count; thus, Fitzsimmons became the new heavyweight champion of the world. It was in this fight in which the solar plexus punch received its first international publicity. Also this fight with Corbett was the first major sports ever to be filmed.

After winning the title, he did not defend it for two years. After the Corbett fight, he made his money in the theater drawing big crowds. Being on a long layoff, he finally decided to fight again, signing to fight Jim Jeffries, a big strong fighter who outweighed Fitz by forty pounds and was thirteen years younger. Fitz took Jeffries lightly, thinking that Jeffries was a big inexperienced fighter, and he never worried about how big a fighter he was. He never thought of himself being rusty, thirty-seven years old, and not the same fighter who beat Corbett for the title two years before.

In the fight with Jim Jeffries, Fitzsimmons lost his title. This, after Fitzsimmons had landed enough punches to whip any ordinary man in the early rounds, and Jeffries just took it and kept coming back. He couldn't find a soft spot on Jeffries saying, "Jim Jeffries had the strength of a bull." After losing his title to Jeffries, Fitzsimmons wanted a rematch with Jeffries. He won five fights by knockouts to get a rematch with Jeffries on July 25, 1902.

In the rematch for nearly eight rounds, it looked as if he would win his title back. Fitzsimmons trained hard for this fight and pounded Jeffries solid throughout the early rounds, but Jeffries being the strong fighter that he is kept coming and taking the punches until he landed a solid left hook to Fitzsimmons's jaw and knocked him out in the eighth round.

After losing the rematch with Jeffries, he admitted that Jeffries was too big and too strong for him to beat. He started going after the light heavyweight title. Being already small, Fitzsimmons had no problem with the weight class; he already had the proper weight. In 1903 Fitzsimmons won the light heavyweight title from George Gardner; on his first defense of his title, he lost his title to Jake O'Brien in the twelfth round in 1905. Fitzsimmons would have his last fight at the age of fifty-two. After his boxing career was over, he appeared on the stage.

Small in size to be considered a heavyweight, he is one of the hardest hitters in the heavyweight history. Looked in size and weight as a light heavyweight or even a middleweight, he knocked out most of all the heavyweights that he fought.

Not only had he killed Riordan in the ring, he also had Jim Corbett almost paralyzed from the waist down for a while by a body punch. In his fight with the original Jack Dempsey, he hit Dempsey in the Adam's apple that impaired Dempsey's speech for life. Fitzsimmons's punching power nearly tore fighters' heads off and broke ribs.

Winning most of his fights by going to the body, his favorite punch was named "the solar plexus punch." It is a punch delivered toward the pit of the stomach, the soft spot on the body. With this punch, he won the heavyweight title and many of his other fights.

In history he was the first fighter to win titles in three different weight divisions. He won the middleweight in 1891, the heavyweight in 1897, and the light heavyweight in 1903.In all he won his first title at the age of twenty-eight and his last at the age of forty-one. Fitzsimmons died in 1917.

James "Jim" Jeffries

JIM
JEFFRIES

Former champion Jim Jeffries strains to see through eyes that are
swollen almost shut as Johnson prepares to attack. When Jeffries,
last hope of the white race, failed to beat the black champion, race
riots erupted throughout the country.

1902: Jim Jeffries and Fitzsimmons before the start of their second fight.
On this occasion, Jeffries, who had won the championship from Fitz in
1899, successfully defended his crown.

James "Jim" Jeffries

Born: 1875-1954, Ohio
Weight: 220 lbs., 6'3"
Champion: 1899-1905

Won: 18   Lost: 1   Drew: 2   Knockouts: 15

In the ring he was Jim Jeffries, one of the strongest heavyweight who ever lived. He could box well and could knockout a man with either hand, and he would never quit.

At 220 pounds, he was the biggest heavyweight of his time. Measured by a doctor, his chest was fifty inches and his waist was thirty inches. Jim was as fast as he was strong. He was clocked running one hundred yards barefoot on turf at eleven seconds.

At the age of twenty years old, he had a job gingerly swinging a ten-pound sledge hammer. It was at this time in 1895 when Jeffries was working at the Punta oil fields in Southern California that he got into boxing. He had no intention of becoming a boxer, but when he was backed into a corner in a con game, he stuck up his dukes. This planted the seed from which James Jeffries grew into the sturdiest fighting oak of all time and became, within four years, heavyweight champion of the world.

It happened as a matter of chance that Hank Griffin, a battle-scared heavyweight long past the twilight of his career, stumbled into the Punta fields one afternoon. Unable to stand up against the professional any longer, Griffin, a Negro, went into business for himself. It was more of a con game than a business because it flourished on man's gullibility and the principle that brains and experience are better than brawn and foolish courage. Griffin moved into the group of well-stacked hotheads and suggested as discreetly as possible that there wasn't a man in the whole bunch brave enough to match punches with him. Griffin had a leather bag filled with twenty-dollar gold pieces in his pocket.

The group matched it and picked Jim Jeffries, the biggest and strongest of the crew being egged into his first official prizefight. Outpointed most of the fight but so strong and able to take punches, Jeffries knocked out Griffin in the fourteenth round. Twelve bouts later, Jim Jeffries would be champion of the world.

Jim was a sparring partner for the top heavyweight contender, including being a sparring partner for Jim Corbett, the heavyweight champion of the world at that time. He helped spar with Corbett for his championship fight with Fitzsimmons in 1897.

Being around Corbett was very helpful to Jeffries. He learned most of his boxing by being a sparring partner of Corbett. With all the science that Jim Corbett knew, it had to rub onto Jeffries.

After training with Corbett, he started on his own career by 1898. Jim had wins over Joe Choynski and Peter Jackson, all top fighters who had fought Corbett but somewhat older.

Jeffries pounded his way through all oppositions without a defeat. At the age of twenty-four and winning his first thirteen fights, he then was pitted with the champion Bob Fitzsimmons. At this time in Jeffries's career, he was still a strong fighter but somewhat a clumsy fighter.

Bob Fitzsimmons, the world champion, had also seen Jeffries's fight and noticed clumsiness and slow movement of Jeffries. Fitzsimmons himself had been out of the ring for two years and wanted an easy fight to start with.

The Fitzsimmons and Jeffries fight took place on June 9, 1899. Not many of the boxing critics gave Jeffries a chance as Fitzsimmons was a heavy betting favorite.

Fitzsimmons fought a good fight and landed some good punches, but Jeffries sulked up all of them. His size, which is about forty pounds difference, was too much for Fitz as he got knocked out in the eleventh round, and a new champion was named Jim Jeffries.

When Jeffries fought he fought fighting from a crouch. With his strength and long reach, it made it very hard to penetrate his guard.

When in his prime, Jeffries made a formidable opponent for any man in the ring, barroom or alleys. Jim believed in his own power, and some people said he had never struck a man with all his force as that would be fatal.

Five years after winning the title, he was still undefeated, beating all contenders, and was impossible to hurt. In his wins, it was six title defenses and none title fights.

Jeffries could hit but could be hit too. In his title defenses, he had some tough fights where he came from behind to win. The fight he had with Tom Sharkey on November 3, 1899, his first defense, went twenty-five rounds where he had to come on strong late in the fight to win on points.

The rematch with Bob Fitzsimmons on July 25, 1902, he took a beating and was behind in points before knocking out Fitzsimmons in the eighth round.

Then when fighting former champion Jim Corbett on May 11, 1900, he was outpointed throughout the fight by Corbett's quickness and was way behind in the fight before coming back in the twenty-third round to win by a knockout.

This goes to show that Jeffries throughout his career was never a clever fighter but always a strong, hard-hitting, take-a-punch, and a very determined fighter.

After being champion for five years and seeing no money fights in what was left of the contenders, Jeffries began talking about retiring from boxing. He said that no living man could defeat him and that no man had ever knocked him to the floor and no man was going too. He had his pride. On that resolution Jeffries announced retirement from the ring on May 13, 1905.

At the time of his retirement, Jeffries had had twenty-two fights, unbeaten in all; but two of them were draws with Joe Choyski and Gus Rulin.

After he retired from the ring as champion, he refereed a match that Marvin Hart won and said that he was the new champion. But it is best to say that the title was vacant and that it was not until Hart had fought Tommy Burns with Burns winning the fight that a true champion was found.

While being retired on his farm from boxing, a black fighter named Jack Johnson was the champion after beating Tommy Burns. The world was looking for a white man to whip the hated black champion. Word went out that Jeffries must emerge from his farm and remove the golden smile from Jack Johnson's face.

Now it appeared to many students of boxing that Johnson had indeed taken away the championship but, instead of earning it for Johnson, had handed it back to James Jeffries. Johnson was to become a no champion, and it was therefore decided that Tommy Burns had been only a custodian of the title rather than a true wearer of the crown. Some of the newspapers began to refer to Jeffries as the undefeated rather than the retired champion, while others called him simply the white heavyweight champion of the world. The racial element, as a consideration in the interpretation of events, was clear.

With all this being said and talked about him, Jim was almost forced to comeback as a white hope to beat the black champion Jack Johnson.

After being retired for five years, Jim agreed to fight Jack Johnson for the championship on July 4, 1910. Jeffries was now thirty-five, and Johnson was twenty-six and in his prime. Being retired so long, Jim had to shed his weight from 315 to 227 pounds.

Jeffries put up a big effort to regain the title for the white race, but he was too far gone and was no match for Johnson. By the thirteenth round, Jeffries was so badly beaten he could barely catch his breath. The crowd began to yell, "Stop It! Don't let him be knocked out!" But the referee allowed the fight to go on, and Johnson kept smashing away.

In the fifteenth Johnson knocked Jeffries half out of the ring. Friends pushed him back. Jeffries collapsed under three snapping blows to the face. The referee counted ten over Jeffries.

In this, his last fight, it was the first time in his life that he had been knocked off his feet and the only fight he lost in his career.

Drunk or sober, Jeffries played the role of heavyweight champion to perfection. In so doing he set the style for Jack Dempsey, the last white heavyweight, to personify raw power in the ring until the appearance of Rocky Marciano and Joe Louis.

Title Vacant: May 13, 1905-February 23, 1906

The first title vacancy started in 1905 when Jim Jeffries retired as the undefeated champion. Jeffries then took it upon himself to stage a fight between a mediocre fighter named Marvin Hart and another uninspired performer named Jack Root.

At the conclusion of the dull bout, Jeffries raised Marvin Hart's hand in token victory and called him the new champion of the world.

The experts didn't take this seriously; Hart and Root were not the best fighters at that time. It was just something that Jim Jeffries took upon himself to do. Even today many references on boxing do not list Marvin Hart as champion.

The experts agreed that when Tommy Burns beat Marvin Hart in 1906, the championship vacancy had been settled. With his wins around the world, he received universal recognition.

Tommy Burns

Tommy Burns (above) stood five feet seven and weighed 180 pounds. He was the ring's shortest champion. Burns held the title from 1906 to 1908.

1908: Tommy Burns attempts a left hook as Jack Johnson toys with him before knocking him out to win the heavyweight title.

Tommy Burns

Born: 1881-1955, Canada
Weight: 180 lbs., 5'7"
Champion: 1906-1908

Won: 46   Lost: 5   Drew: 9   Knockouts: 37

Tommy Burns was the first, what you would call, a fighting champion. He fought often, and he fought the best there was. In 1908 he defended his title seven times; at five feet seven, he was the shortest of all the heavyweight champions. Although small, Burns was a superb boxing strategist, he had to be when he fought bigger men. With a boxing weight of 180 pounds, he was fast and had great stamina, along with the ability to strike a disintegrating blow.

Living in Detroit and working, he joined the Detroit Athletic Club to stay in shape. Burns learned his boxing at this Detroit Athletic Club. At the club he would start his boxing career; he would also have his first professional fight at nineteen years of age at the club, winning by a knockout. He would go on and win the Michigan middleweight championship.

He was christened Noah Brusso and used the name Tommy Burns from a jockey when he went into prizefighting. Being small, Burns started his career in 1900s as a welterweight. As he continued to fight, Burns began to gain weight; and by 1905 weighing 175 pounds, he began to fight as a heavyweight fighter. He had great success as a welterweight, middleweight, and as a heavyweight fighter. Fighting professional Burns did good, winning twenty-nine of thirty-fights with twenty-one knockouts.

After Jim Jeffries retired from the ring as the undefeated champion of the world, he decided that a match between Marvin Hart and Jack Root would determine who the next heavyweight champion would be. Hart won by a knockout to claim to be the champion, and Jim Jeffries said that Hart was the new heavyweight champion.

Most boxing fans did not go along with Hart being the new champion or with what Jeffries had said that Hart was the new champion. The people did not go along with this fight for the championship because at the time of the Marvin Hart and Jack Root fight for the title, Hart was just an average fighter and Root was a light heavyweight fighter.

With Burns's great success, now fighting as a heavyweight, the boxing world wanted Marvin Hart to fight Tommy Burns to determine a real champion. On February 23, 1906, Burns got the chance to fight Marvin Hart who Jim Jeffries had said was the champion for the title. Most boxing people and fans believed that this fight between Marvin Hart and Tommy Burns would settle who the real champion since Jim Jeffries had retired as champion from the ring.

Burns won the fight over Hart by points in twenty rounds and became the champion. By winning the title, by not beating the recognized champion but winning it in a preliminary fight, Burns had to prove himself to the public that he was a champion.

A month after winning the championship, he had two exhibition fights in the same night when he beat both Jim Walter and Jim O'Brien by knockouts in the first round. In Burns's first defense of his title, he fought Jim Flynn. In this fight, Flynn was very tough on Burns, winning the early rounds and giving Burns a bad beating. Burns would show how tough he was by coming back and winning on a fifteen-round knockout.

Before Burns became champion, he fought a draw with the veteran Philadelphian Jack O'Brien. After winning the title, they would fight two more times. O'Brien was the light heavyweight champion at the time. The second fight went to a twenty-round draw that most people thought Burns had won. In the third fight between Burns and O'Brien, Burns won an easy fight. By beating O'Brien, Burns was now also the light heavyweight champion. Burns didn't want the light heavyweight title, so he gave it up.

After defeating the American fighters, Burns went on a world tour to fight the champions and top fighters in foreign countries. He did this for a year and a half. He went to Australia where he knocked out Jewey Smith, the Australian champion, in thirteen rounds, and went to England and defeated the English champion Gunner Moir in ten rounds, and went to Ireland and knocked out the Irish champion Jem Roche in one round.

Burns was boastful, cocky, tough, and would belittle other fighters. When English reporters asked him for his opinion of the British champion Gunner Moir, he said, "The guy is a bum." Leaving social questions aside, Burns was the sort of champion the sporting public liked because everything he did, from his bragging in the press to his followers, was predictable.

In all Burns had eight wins in his year and a half world tour and won fourteen fights since winning the title from Hart two years before; during this time Burns was getting constant challenges by Jack Johnson to fight him for the title.

By now it was known that Burns was a true world champion by everyone — everybody except for Jack Johnson, a black fighter who began following Burns around on his world tour demanding a shot at the title. Burns continued to fight everyone except Johnson.

As time went by, Burns decided the time at last or was forced to fight Johnson on December 26, 1908. This was the fight the international sporting public most wanted to see. Until this time in boxing, no black man had ever fought for the title. Burns was to change that when he signed to fight Jack Johnson. Burns went back to his bragging, making statements about "Jack's yellow streak." "I'll fight him and whip him as sure as my name is Tommy Burns."

Even though Burns was giving up twenty pounds in weight and six inches in height, Burns was a slight favorite. Tommy, as being the champion, got a record $30,000 for the fight, which was a record, and drew a gate of $121,000, which also was a record.

By the end of the first round, everybody who was at the fight knew that Burns was outmatched and had no chance of beating Johnson. Nothing he could do could match the perfect defense and boxing skills of Johnson. Not once in fourteen rounds did he ever hurt Johnson, and he became very frustrated at his inability to hurt Johnson. Burns was so tough that many paid customers thought that Tommy may last the full twenty rounds.

Johnson toyed with Burns and could have put Burns out early anytime in the fight. In the fourteenth round, Johnson knocked Burns down for the count of eight; when Burns struggled to his feet, he was dazed and defenseless, and the police entered the ring to save him from injury. As soon as Burns got his breath, he began to curse the officers and shout that he wasn't licked, but it was over. Burns would say later in his life that in the Johnson fight, he was coming on stronger and that Johnson was weaker as the fight went on.

Burns continued to fight off and on for the next twelve years with some success. His last fight was in 1920 against Joe Beckett, and he was knocked out in seven rounds. Fighting for twenty years, Burns never had a manager. He had his own fights, trained as he wanted to, and kept his own accounts.

Tommy Burns would never be remembered up there with the top heavyweight champions of all time but as an aggressive, good fighter. He fought and won often when he was champion. Burns also was the only champion that went and fought all the champions in other countries. It must be understood that the years he was champion, the contender to the title wasn't good; only Jack Johnson was a class opponent, and he had to wait almost two years for Burns to fight him.

In 1948 Burns became a minister, and he stated that in his fighting days he had been "vicarious and full of hatred." This was particularly so at the time he fought Johnson; as he put it, "Race prejudices was rampant in my mind. The idea of a black man challenging me was beyond enduring. Hatred made me tense; it wasn't Johnson who beat Tommy Burns, but Tommy Burns beating who beat himself."

Burns died in May of 1955 of a heart attack. He was seventy-three years old.

Jack Johnson

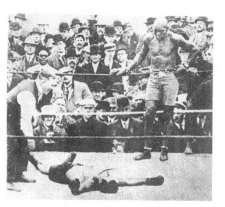

Johnson stares at Stanley Ketchel's outstretched body after knocking him out in the twelfth round. This was Johnson's first defense of his title, October 16, 1909.

Johnson watches Jim Jeffries collapse during championship bout in 1910.

Jack Johnson, the great black world heavyweight champion

Young mourner pays his last respects to boxing great at funeral at Chicago's Pilgrim Baptist Church.

Johnson collected hundreds of speeding tickets throughout his lifetime. Note officer's bike.

Johnson breaks down Burns—and a racial barrier.

Standing on the Mexican border, Johnson shakes hands with deputy sheriff of Imperial County, California, before ending his exile.

Etta Duryea, first of his three white wives, at the time of their marriage in 1911

Jack Johnson, age sixty-seven, prepares for boxing exhibition at a New York war-bond rally in 1945.

Jack Johnson

Born: 1878-1946; Galveston, Texas
Weight: 200 lbs., 6′ 2″
Champion: 1908-1915

Won: 86   Lost: 10   Drew: 11   Knockouts: 40

Jack Johnson was the first black world heavyweight champion. Many people acknowledged him to be the finest fighting machine who ever lived. He was also the most colorful, most independent, most confident, most flamboyant, and most controversial whoever laced on gloves.

Johnson was a black crusader. He crusaded in his own unique way by thumbing his nose at the white man and hitting him in his most vulnerable spot, the white women.

While growing up in Galveston, Texas, he became aware of his boxing talent at an early age. He saw that he had speed, and along with that he had been endowed with an easy natural boxing style. One fight complemented the other.

Jack left school after the fifth grade to find work. At intervals he would work at Professor Herman Bernau's sporting gymnasium as a janitor. Professor Bernau allowed Johnson to punch the bag after hours and exercise with the weights. He also had the privilege of buying two pairs of boxing gloves at the wholesale price. He carried these gloves around the Negro section of Galveston.

At his gathering place, Johnson would walk up to a man, throw him one pair of gloves, and start putting on the other. This was the signal for an informal boxing bout in which Jack always delighted the spectators while rapidly taking the heart out of his opponent.

Johnson began to think about making money from his quickness of foot and his ability to strike a paralyzing blow with either hand. At this time Bob Tomlinson, a professional boxer turned circus roustabout, traveled through Texas in the spring of 1897 with a carnival troupe and picked up easy money by fighting all comers in a tented ring. With spectators at fifty cents a head, Tomlinson offered five dollars to anyone who could stay four rounds with him. Few of the farm boys, ranch hands, and saloon fighters who tried for this prize survived even one round; and none had ever been upright at the end of four. Jack accepted his invitation to enter the ring. As Johnson climbed through the ropes, Tomlinson sized him up as stupid but strong. A gong sounded; Johnson came from his corner in a loose, jointed, shuffling way that caught the attention of the audience. Tomlinson decided to keep Johnson going for three rounds to please the crowd.

If anyone was carried along, it was Tomlinson. Jack avoided his rushes with ease or tied him up at close quarters, smiling all the while. In the fourth round, Johnson whipped over a belly punch that made his eyes bug. Bent and gasping, Tomlinson was barely able to last till the bell. The five dollars, thereupon collected, was the first that he earned with his fighting skills.

On his climb to the title, he was traveling around the states to fights; he took part in battle royal. This form of contest had six men enter the ring and swing away until only one was on his feet. He later worked with the original Joe Walcott. Walcott gave Johnson his first employment as a professional boxer in a recognized troupe by adding him to the corps of sparring partners. Walcott helped polish his fighting style. With his own natural rhythm, Walcott was a fine instructor for Johnson, teaching him graceful movement that was a kind of art.

Jack was born in Galveston, Texas, in 1878. At the height of his professional career, he was six feet two and weighing a little over two hundred pounds. His head was always shaven skin clean and his face was strong, sturdy, and well fleshed.

Johnson was very easily the greatest defensive heavyweight boxer who ever lived. He relied primarily on orthodox boxing, which he carried to near perfection. Completely he had mastered all aspects of the style. Jack was especially adept at feinting and counterpunching. His defense relied heavily on the art of blocking and, if necessary, remained stationary and not get hit. It was this perfected ability that kept him from taking any beating, even long after the spring in his legs was gone. The average slow-moving, slow-thinking heavyweight was like a child in Jack's hands. Being a master boxer, he fought flat-footed, shuffling around the ring rather awkwardly, which concealed the real speed of his movements. He never allowed himself to be hurried, conserving his resources of strength until the time came for the kill. When his fighting days would be over, he left the ring unmarked and unscarred.

Johnson started fighting professionally in 1897. He almost immediately became a contender. In 1901 Jack lost by a third-round knockout to Joe Chynski. He did not lose another fight until March 28, 1905 when he lost a controversial decision to Marvin Hart. Everybody who was at the fight was shocked at the decision. Jack had knocked Hart out of the ring in an earlier round.

From 1902 up until 1908, Johnson won most of his fights rather easily, but the champion before him gave him the runaround. Jack wanted a shot at the title held by Jim Jeffries but never had the chance as Jeffries retired undefeated in 1905. After Tommy Burns became champion in 1906, he made Johnson wait two more years before getting a shot at the title.

The most difficult thing that Jack seemed to have in the ring was his color. The white promoters ran everything. The whites only wanted them to be beaten or fighting amongst their own race. If they were too good, especially in the heavyweight division, a color line was drawn to stop them from fighting and beating the white champion. The case of John L. Sullivan's refusal to fight the top contender Peter Jackson, who was black, was an example of this.

At the time many boxing fans and people in general approved of anything that would prevent Jack from achieving success and fame. The greater part of his resentment came from his preference for the company of white women. They resented Johnson seeking out these white women and escorting them to places of public entertainment. He later would have three white wives.

There were other ways he could excite indignation by making people angry from the expression on his face, taunting his opponents, and by the manner in which he went about his fights. Because he was such a good fighter, sometimes he would hold back, which caused the crowd to become angry at him for not extending himself.

What happened to Peter Jackson seemed to happen to Johnson. Over ten years he defeated top contenders easily with hardly any chance to fight for the title. But Jack wanted to fight for the championship held by Tommy Burns badly, and he wouldn't give up.

When Tommy Burns went on a world tour, Johnson was right on his heels issuing challenges at every stop, demanding a title fight. Jack finally got his chance as Burns agreed to fight him on December 26, 1908.

Jack disliked Burns for different reasons. Before the fight Burns made a statement about Jack having a yellow streak saying, "I will bet a few plunks that the colored man will not make good." Jack also disliked Burns because he had to chase him all around the world to get a title fight with him.

In the fight Johnson masterfully knocked out Burns in the fourteenth round. He probably could have done away with him sooner. Throughout the fight he taunted Burns, "Who told you I was yellow?," telling Burns, "You ain't showed me nothing yet."

After winning the title from Burns, a cry went up for a great white hope to beat the new black champion. It was laid mostly on the former undefeated champion Jim Jeffries.

His trouble began after he became champion in beating Burns in 1908. When he stepped into the ring, he was cursed, and they tried to trip him as he walked down the aisle. They threw cigar butts and bottles at him when he won.

Jack started living in high fashion and married a white woman. By this time there was general gripping about Johnson's behavior. A cry went up to find a great white hope. The pressure was put on old Jim Jeffries, the ex-champ, to come out of retirement and meet Johnson.

Johnson and Jeffries met July 4, 1910. It was no contest with Johnson's superiority, he kidded and taunted Jeffries and chatted with the referee. He put Jeffries out in the fifteenth round.

The white-hope search really got into full force after Johnson's triumph over Jim Jeffries. The repercussions from Jeffries downfall were something to behold. A frenzied scramble started to find a fighter capable of whipping Johnson and redeeming the honor and prestige of the white race. Promoters and managers scoured the highways and byways of the world for a fighter to beat Johnson. Any big guy who looked as though he could fight at all was a natural prospect. The hectic hunt reached to farms and factories, to cattle ranges and coal mines, to river docks and lumber camps. White-hope tournaments popped up all over the landscape.

After Jack became champion, he continued to whip white fighters. He was reluctant to defend his title against men of his own race. Before he became champion, he fought black fighters, and they were his toughest fights.

At the time Johnson was champion, there were top black fighters like Sam Langford, Joe Jeanette, Sam McVey, and Harry Wills. Most of them were tough fights he had with them on his way up to the title and all wins for Johnson. During this time, with Jim Jeffries being retired, the white race had no great fighters. The black fighters, Langford, Jeanette, and McVey, were far superior but couldn't get a shot at Johnson's title.

In-between fights, Jack continued to get into trouble with the law, overspeeding tickets and his association with white women. Jack said he couldn't get along with Negro women because he couldn't trust them.

Johnson was disliked by a lot of his black race and by all whites while being champion. He was by far the most hated fighter in heavyweight history. Some blacks did not approve of Johnson's conduct. Booker T. Washington, a former slave, founder of Tuskegee Institute, and knowledgeable spokesman for American Negroes, joined in the criticism of Johnson. Washington said, "Jack Johnson has harmed rather than helped the black race. I wish to say emphatically that his actions do not meet my approval and I'm sure they do not meet with the approval of the colored race." With the problems of his habits of life, drinking, and gambling, leaving the color aside, Johnson was not the likeable person to look up to. Johnson collected white girlfriends and wives the way some people collected coins. He was always in court for it.

While running a place called the Cafe'de Champion, a place of entertainment in 1913, Jack was charged with the Mann Act. This was a law that forbade interstate transportation of women for immoral purposes. He went to court May 13, 1913, before a jury and Judge Carpenter; took the stand in his own defense, and denied the charge of the Mann Act. Even though there was no evidence that Jack had violated it, he was convicted. Johnson got his sentencing June 4, 1913. Judge Carpenter said the crime, which the defendant was guilty of, was an aggravating one; and the life of the defendant had been such as to merit condemnation.

The judge sentenced Johnson to one year and one day in the Joilet Penitentiary plus a fine of one thousand dollars. He then granted two weeks of execution to give time to have Johnson's conviction reversed in the circuit court of appeals. During these fourteen days, Johnson would remain free.

Johnson, with his ingrained lifestyle, could not accept the idea that he would go to prison. He believed that he would not be sentenced to prison if his skin had been white. He wasn't worried about the one-thousand-dollar fine because that was a small lot to him. What he was worried about was a year out of the ring, now that his earning power was at its high. With all this on his mind, he decided to jump bail. In order to avoid prison, Johnson fled the country and went into a self-imposed exile to live in Europe in 1913. At the time he began his exile, he was thirty-five years old.

While in exile he did a lot of different jobs, traveling on tours and performing different acts. In a lot of places he was not welcomed because of his white-slave agitation rising from the trial in the States. Johnson would say his real crime was beating Jim Jeffries.

Jack won two fights while in exile that he had not trained for. One was a draw with a black fighter named Jim Johnson in December 1913 in Paris, France. In the fight Jack broke his left hand and was unable to continue. The referee declared the fight a draw after ten rounds. This was the first time in heavyweight history that it was an all-Negro world heavyweight title bout.

Jack's other win was over Frank Moran in June 1914 in Paris, France. Jack won the fight on points over Moran in twenty rounds. Jack was in poor condition for these wins over Jim Johnson and Frank Moran, with his superior defense holding up.

Two years after being in exile, he signed to meet big Jess Willard, one of the better white hopes, for the title. Willard stood six feet six tall, weighed 250 pounds. Johnson knew the fight would draw a good payday.

Johnson and Willard were signed to fight in Havana, Cuba, on April 5, 1915. Jack was thirty-seven years old. By this time in Jack's career, his eating and drinking were well over what it should be. He was well past his prime. Willard on the other hand trained hard for the title shot.

It was a very hot day for the fight. The heat seemed to affect Johnson more than Willard. By the eighth round, Johnson was gasping and panting. The high point for Johnson was in round thirteen where he pummeled Willard but did not knock him down. Nine rounds later Johnson was hanging on as the crowd yelled for Willard to finish Johnson off. Willard knocked out Johnson in the twenty-sixth round. After leaving the ring, Johnson said, "Willard was too much for me. I just didn't have it."

Johnson had said that on the subject of white hope, the crusade to find a white man who could beat him carried on so bitterly and intensely that it caused him much trouble, sorrow, and persecution. He said it only ended after he lost his title to Willard and that nobody was more relieved than he was when it finally ended.

Jack thought he could get a remission of his jail term now that Willard had the championship, so Johnson wrote his Chicago lawyers. They wrote back saying he would go to prison if he returned to the United States. For the next five years, he became hard to handle and occasionally dangerous; he thought he was let down.

As an ex-champion in exile, he fought some, even though he didn't take boxing seriously, fighting no bodies. He also did some bullfighting and promotional fights without too much success. His mind was on returning to the United States. His mother died in 1917. Still young he did not want to spend the rest of his life in exile.

Johnson surrendered to Federal men on July 20, 1920, saying, "I've come back to straighten out that mix-up with the government and look up that fellow, what's his name Dempsey?"

He went to court September 14, 1920, and had the same judge, Carpenter. Judge Carpenter said, "Johnson has behaved in a manner to indicate a complete disregard for the laws and institutions of this country." With that he ordered Jack to the Federal penitentiary at Leavenworth, Kansas, to serve out his time of one year and a day.

Johnson was released on July 9, 1921. In his later years, he always tried to make a fortune. He always managed to keep a roof over his head, good clothes, and a fast car to drive. He appeared in traffic courts regularly. When he died in 1946, he was speeding and hit a lamp pole. He was sixty-eight years old. He was still giving exhibitions up to the age of sixty-seven.

Criticism of Johnson's behavior outside the ring undoubtedly was based on the color of his skin. There were white champions, then and later, who were less than models of modesty. But Johnson's era was marked by persecution of blacks in general, and the world was not ready for him. Johnson had probably the best defense of any champion and still a great boxer. He had knockout power in either hand. He is the only champion to have all of these mastered.

In 1927 he got the recognition he had long wished for. The official publication on boxing was the magazine, *The Ring*, and in 1927 it stated that "Jack Johnson was the greatest heavyweight of all time." The editor and publisher of *The Ring* was Nat Fleischer and generally regarded as the sport's most authoritative historian.

Nat Fleischer said this because Johnson achieved the highest rating of all the heavyweight champions in all-around ability, feinting, hitting, blocking, and counterpunching. He was also big and strong. Fleischer said, "After years devoted to the study of heavyweight fighters, I have no hesitation in naming Jack Johnson as the greatest of them all."

Jess Willard

Jess Willard was tall! At 6'6 ½," he was the tallest heavyweight champion in history. He is best remembered for defeating Jack Johnson in a title fight in Havana, Cuba.

The end of one of the most controversial fights of all time, Jack Johnson vs. Jess Willard Johnson, while being counted out, seems to be shading his eyes from the blazing Cuban sun.

Willard training for fight with Dempsey with sparring partner Walter Monaba

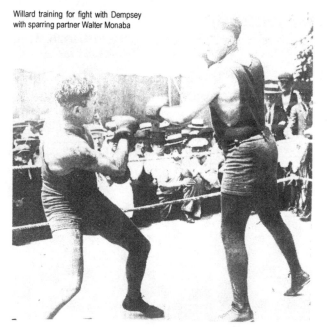

Jess Willard

Born: 1881-1968, Kansas
Weight: 243 lbs., 6'6"
Champion: 1915-1919

Won: 28   Lost: 6   Drew: 1   Knockout: 21

At six feet six, Jess Willard was the tallest heavyweight champion in history. Fighting at around 250 pounds, he was one of the heaviest champions of all. Willard was remarkably fast for a man his size and had good power. As for courage Jess was one of the bravest of all champions. He had a very effective left jab because of his big reach of eighty-three inches. Willard's jab was often good enough to win him the fights.

Before becoming a fighter, Willard was a farm boy who broke horses and worked the farm. During this time he never thought about boxing, could care less that the champion was a black man named Jack Johnson, or even care less that a search was out to find a great white hope to beat and take the title from the hated black champion Jack Johnson.

It was here on the farm where he got into boxing. People who saw him on the farm, and saw how big he was, encourage Willard to try to be a fighter, where he could make more money than working on the farm. It was here where he began doing his early fighting in the stable. He soon left the farm to have a boxing career.

Willard left and went to Oklahoma City where he met his manager Tom Jones. Starting late for a fighter, Willard didn't have his first fight until he was twenty-eight years old in 1911. By now he knew of the big money that was made in the ring and figured with his big size and strength, he could make it.

Starting his career in 1911, he had a lot of wins. A lot of his wins were because he had long arms, with his arms so long he could keep fighters off of him with an effect jab. While Jack Johnson was still the champion, early in Willard's career he was told he was to be the great white hope, saying it was his patriotic duty to restore the heavyweight championship to the white race. After winning most of his fights in Oklahoma, he then left to make bigger money. Leaving Oklahoma, Willard went to Chicago where he met a former fighter named Charles Cutter. Cutter taught Willard the finer points of boxing. Willard had good success in Chicago getting some knockout wins. Then he was off to New York.

Fighting in New York, Jess did okay. Then in May 1913, Willard lost a twenty-round decision to a hard-hitting fighter named Gunboat Smith. This loss caused him to lose prestige as a white hope.

In August of the same year, he knocked out Bull Young in eleven rounds. Jess won the fight with a roundhouse right. Young went into a coma and later died. This hurt Willard a lot because he was an easygoing fighter who didn't want to hurt anyone. This also caused him to hold back in some fights. Jess even wanted to quit after this fight but was told he was the great white hope.

Jess continued to fight and win, even though some of his fights were boring to the fans. He then lay off from the ring for a year to do nothing but rest. While being out of the ring, his manager got in touch with the promoter and then with Jess to let him know that he had a chance to fight Jack Johnson for the title. By the time the fight was signed, Big Jess was weighing 320 pounds. He trained hard for this once-in-a-lifetime fight. His weight went down, and he was in the best shape ever for this fight.

Johnson and Willard fought on April 5, 1915. In fighting Johnson, Willard fought a safe, cautious fight. The fight was rather even for twenty rounds. Willard took advantage of his eighty-four-inch reach. Johnson gave Willard his best; at thirty-seven he lost too much power. Willard fought steady and wore Johnson down. By the twenty-sixth round, Johnson had no defense. Willard moved in and knocked out Johnson with a punch to the chin.

Before he beat Jack Johnson for the title, there were a lot of other great white hopes who had tried to win the title but failed.

After Willard beat Johnson, he was called the great white hope who made good. After beating Johnson, he became a national hero. He drew big crowds everywhere he went. Willard made good money with his popularity, touring the country with the circuses and the Buffalo Bill's Wild, Wild West Show. With the Wild Wild West Show, he made between $1,000 to $2,500 a day.

As a champion Willard was not a fighting champion. He didn't fight for a year after winning the title. His first defense was against Frank Moran on March 25, 1916. Willard fought a dull fight but won a ten-round decision over Moran. Three years went by before Willard defended his title again. During this time he did some exhibitions and other engagements on stage. In all, Willard defended his title only two times in the four years he was champion.

Willard was probably the least of all the champions not to have his heart into the fighting game. Even when he was the champion, he said he did not like fighting or hurting people. He showed it in his style of fighting where he loafed along and only extended himself enough to win. For being as big as he was, he never had the killer attack in him in the ring. He mostly used his jabs.

After three years of no title fight, promoter Tex Richard signed Willard to fight Jack Dempsey for the title on July 4, 1919. Going into the fight with Jack Dempsey, Willard was out of shape with excess of fat; he didn't train hard, and he thought that Dempsey had no chance of winning his title. In this championship fight against Dempsey, Willard was thirty-eight years old. He towered over the shorter Jack Dempsey, but the excess fat on his body was obvious.

In the Willard and Dempsey fight, Willard was totally outmatched against Dempsey. Willard proved to the boxing world that he was no quitter as he was knocked down seven times in the first round and was repeatedly hit hard, but continue to get up and take more punishment. The second and third rounds were the same as Dempsey fought furiously, throwing power punches to Willard's body that was literally broken apart. In the start of the fourth round, Willard was unable to come out to fight because his crushed ribs threatened his lung; he couldn't breathe. His chief second threw in the towel, losing his title.

After the fight was stopped, Willard had to be led back to his dressing room because his eyes were so swollen. In losing his title to Dempsey in this fight, Willard suffered a fractured cheekbone, front teeth were knocked out, and six of his ribs were broken and caved in; and he lost a lot of blood. In this fight with Dempsey, he would not give up, despite the beating he took.

This is probably the worst beating any heavyweight champion had ever taken in a ring, before Willard or after Willard. Because of this fight, he is looked at as one of the bravest and showed more courage than any champion had showed in the ring, as he kept fighting, getting up, and not giving up. Willard contested all his life that Dempsey's gloves were loaded and contained something other than the usual padding.

After losing his title to Dempsey, Willard retired from the ring. He then made a comeback after four years, hoping to get a rematch with Dempsey for the title and to make some money. On May 12, 1923, Willard signed to fight Floyd Johnson. In the fight Willard surprised everyone by knocking out Johnson in the eleventh round.

Willard would end his boxing career in his last fight also in 1923 when he fought Luis Firpo. Fighting an okay fight with Firpo, he won some rounds before his age would show as he tired and his legs got tired and was knocked out in the eighth round. For the Firpo fight, Willard was forty-one years old.

Jess Willard was one of the most underrated heavyweight champion of all times. Lots of people would say that the only way he became champion was because Jack Johnson didn't train right, was out of shape, and too old. They would also say that he was just an average fighter who was only a big heavyweight fighter for his enormous size but lacked a killer instinct and boxing ability, and he was awkward.

Jack Johnson was one of the main reasons boxing people didn't think much of Willard as a fighter. Johnson had said five years after their fight that he took a dive, threw the fight to hand the title to Willard on a deal. He said also that he could have knocked Willard out anytime he wanted to in the fight. Hearing about this, Willard would say, "Why did he wait twenty-six rounds under a sun that was 115 degrees hot to quit? Or wait five years to say he took a dive?"

Years later after people who knew boxing studied the Willard and Johnson fight, they found out that Willard was a much better fighter than he was given credit for. The thing that Jess Willard will always be remembered for most is that he was the only great white hope who made good in 1915, finally beating and ending the championship reign of the black heavyweight champion Jack Johnson.

Jack Dempsey

5. Carpentier falls in fourth round, July 2, 1921.
6. Tommy Gibbons (left) lasted fifteen rounds.
7. Jack doesn't give Luis Firpo a chance to recover.
8. Training for first Tunney fight, 1926
9. Jack loses title to Tunney (rt), Phila.
10. Jack Sharkey, a Dempsey kayo victim, poses with Jack in his NY restaurant.

1. First known photo of Jack in fighting pose was taken in Victor, Colorado, about 1912.
2. With manager Jack Kearns, Dempsey arrives in New York City for bout with Bert Kenny, 1916.
3. Moments before Dempsey kayoed towering Fred Fulton at Harrison, New Jersey, in 1918
4. Dempsey and champion Jess Willard posed before historic bout at Toledo, Ohio, on July 4, 1919. Third-round kayo gave Jack title.
5. Jack (rt) kayoed Bill Brennen in 1920 title bout.
6. Sparring with lightweight Joe Benjamin in 1922
7. Dempsey made Hollywood debut in 1923.

Jack Dempsey

Born: 1895-1983; Manassas, Colorado
Weight: 189 lbs., 6'1"
Champion: 1919-1926

Won: 64   Lost: 6   Drew: 9   Knockouts: 49

Talking about Jack Dempsey, people are talking about one of the most idolized athletes who ever lived, the first ring idol since John L. Sullivan was champion and the greatest terror the heavyweight division had ever seen. All heavyweight champions, past and present, are compared to Dempsey, what they could have done.

In size Dempsey was kind of small, weighing 189 pounds, but he had a rock for a jaw and a fist as hard as a rock.

When Jack fought, he was a no-nonsense slugger. Being a pure slugger, he liked to get it over with fast. Once the bell rang in the first round, he would be a vicious terror trying to tear his opponent apart by mauling them, by beating the body with a right to the body and left hook to the chin for the knockout.

Dempsey's punch was so devastating that few fighters could stand with him. A fierce, two-fisted, attack was how he always fought and got adopted by a nation during the golden age of the 1920s.

In the beginning he had an ordinary career of fighting all over the country: in coal mines, saloons, and fighting lumber jacks. It was fighting in these places that Jack got noticed for his boxing power ability and getting the reputation of being a knockout artist.

Growing up in Manassas, Colorado, Jack was the ninth of eleven children born to Hyrum and Celia Dempsey. Growing up in Manassas, he got into boxing at an early age by reading a book that was in his house on the biography life story of the former great heavyweight champion John L. Sullivan. Having this book around him all the time, he too wanted to be a fighter and a champion like the great John L. Sullivan.

Living on the farm, he would build his own punching bag with sand and punch it until his hands were sore. By the age of sixteen, Dempsey was getting fights; by this time he already knew he was going to be a professional fighter.

Still young Dempsey had regular jobs. He moved to West Virginia where he worked digging coal. Doing this type of work is very hard, but it would help Dempsey later in his life because it builds up the body. When he turned to fighting full time, this work in the coal mines built up his arms and shoulder muscle that would later generate raw power.

Dempsey's early years as a fighter was tough, and he was tough; while fighting he worked the mines, picked fruits, slept on benches, jumped freight cars to get to fights, had his manager skip town with all the money, struggling for food and just living off the land. He was a very determined fighter.

The early part of his career, he would also go through a lot of managers. A lot of them did not have Dempsey's best interest; they just wanted the money they would make off him. Before Dempsey was ready to fight the top contender, they wanted him to fight Sam Langford. At the time the other fighters didn't want to fight the tough black fighter Langford who maybe was the best fighter of all at that time. Dempsey was wise enough to know he wasn't ready for Sam Langford, and he let them know.

Things began to click for Dempsey in San Francisco when Jack Kearns took over as his manager. Kearns knew all about the fight game and dealing with promoters. Dempsey and Kearns had immediate success.

Kearns got Dempsey a fight with Carl Morris. It was only a four-round bout; only four rounds were allowed in California at the time. Morris was the first prominent heavyweight brought in to meet Jack. This was in 1917.

It was the decision he pounded out over Morris that actually started Dempsey on his drive to the world championship.

In 1917 Dempsey got knocked out by Jim Flynn. Flynn was a veteran fighter who had fought and lost a chance to win the title from Jack Johnson in 1912. In the Jim Flynn-Dempsey fight,

Dempsey got knocked down four times in the first round, as his corner men threw in the towel to end it. The knockout when Dempsey lost to Flynn would be the only time Dempsey would ever be knocked out. Jack got revenge against Flynn the following year when he knocked Flynn out in seven rounds.

During Dempsey's climb to the title, there was a navy fighter named Willie Meehan who always gave Jack trouble. Meehan was a sailor who was built like a roly-poly heavyweight. He and Meehan had a series of fights. At this time, Dempsey was a hungry savage brawler whose mere appearance in the ring was terrifying. The mighty Dempsey was never able to do anything with the shifty Willie Meehan. The last of their three meetings took place in San Francisco in 1918 and resulted in a decision for Meehan.

This was at a time when Dempsey was fresh off a surge of spectacular knockout in eastern rings. It appeared that he had Jack's number. The next year Dempsey would be world champion.

The year 1918 was a very busy and successful year for Dempsey. He had a total of twenty-two fights, winning all of them except the one lost to Willie Meehan. He would score seventeen knockouts. The wins in 1918 were over some of the top fighters like Fred Fulton, Battling Levinsky, Carl Morris, and Gunboat Smith. Kearns knew that his fighter was now ready to fight the champion Jess Willard.

Willard was willing to fight Dempsey for the championship on July 4, 1919; he hadn't fought in a long time, and he thought this was a fight he could win. Hardly anybody gave Dempsey a chance in this fight against the gigantic Jess Willard. The promoter Tex Rickard didn't want the fight, saying Dempsey was too small. For this fight Willard was six feet six tall to the six feet one Dempsey, and Willard weighed in at 245 to Dempsey's 187 pounds.

In the fight Dempsey destroyed Willard of encaged ferocity that caused even harden ringsiders to look the other way. Dempsey was throwing such hard punches with both hands into Willard's head and body. Punches were ripping from everywhere; Willard was helpless as Dempsey knocked him to the floor seven times in the first round. After three brutal rounds, Dempsey won the fight in the fourth round.

In 1920 Dempsey would have two defenses of his title. He would win a three-round knockout over Billy Miskee and a twenty-round knockout over Bill Brennan.

On July 2, 1921, promoter Tex Rickard set up a fight between Dempsey and Georges Carpentier as the fight of the century. Dempsey won the fight by a fourth-round knockout of Carpentier. This would be boxing's first million-dollar gate.

Dempsey's manager Kearns and promoter Rickard wanted another million dollars' gate for Dempsey's next title fight. They choose to fight Luis Firpo. Firpo had already defeated a top contender in Bill Brennan and also had defeated the former world heavyweight champion Jess Willard. Firpo was bigger and taller than Dempsey. Rickard and Kearns thought that Firpo was the right contender to bring them another million-dollar gate. Both of them also knew that Firpo was a dangerous fighter to the title.

On September 14, 1923, Dempsey and Luis Firpo, "the Wild Bull of the Pampas" fought. A crowd of eighty-two thousand fans poured into New York Polo Grounds to see a short but violent two-round fight that many still believe was the most exciting fight in heavyweight history. This would be the second million-dollar fight in boxing history. The Dempsey and Firpo fight would make $1,188,603 dollars.

The massive Firpo took a horrible beating. In the first round Dempsey knocked Firpo down seven times, and two times in the second round from Jack's sweeping left hooks and pile-driving rights. Eight times Firpo managed to get to his feet with Dempsey standing over him, ready to pound him again.

What made the fight memorable happened late in round one when Firpo's uppercut sent Jack sprawling out of the ring onto a writer's typewriter. It took the efforts of three men to shove Dempsey back into the ring to be able to beat the count and save his title. Firpo would knock Dempsey down two times total. For a fight that lasted only two rounds, it had the action of a fight that went the distance.

The fight with Firpo would be Jack's last title fight for the next three years. For three years he sat on his title, boxed exhibitions, traveled around the country, getting a little heavier and a few years older. Jack held the title for almost seven years, but he defended it only five times.

In September of 1926, Dempsey defended his title against Gene Tunney. He was now thirty-one years old after being out so long. Tunney was a skilled fighter, but the betting was that Dempsey the slugger could beat Tunney the boxer.

In fighting Tunney, Dempsey's inactivity showed in his fighting power and fighting spirit, and you could tell that his peak years had passed.

Tunney skillfully but unspectacularly outboxed Dempsey throughout ten rounds and took his title. Only once in the fight, in the fourth round, did Jack threaten. His left hook shook Tunney, and when his knees buckled, Tunney had to hold the top rope with his right hand to steady himself.

Instead of following through, Jack backed away. Three years out of the ring had slowed his reflexes. He was a marked man for Tunney's jarring left and heavy-handed right crosses. Dempsey was 11-5 favorite going in, but the result was inevitable.

The fight was fought in Philadelphia and was the largest attended prizefight. The record gathering numbered 120,757.

In those days former champions, even Jack Dempsey, didn't get another crack at the title unless they earned it. Because Jack was so badly beaten by Tunney, he had to show that he was worthy of a rematch with Tunney. Dempsey agreed to fight anybody to get a rematch against Tunney. And so Dempsey signed to fight Jack Sharkey on July 21, 1927. Dempsey won by a knockout in the seventh round, setting the stage for a rematch with Tunney.

Dempsey and Tunney were signed to battle at Chicago Soldiers Field the following year, 1927. It drew a crowd of 105,000 and the biggest gate, $2,658,660. Everybody wanted to know if Dempsey had enough left to catch up to the fast moving Tunney.

The rematch is better known as the Long Count Fight. Tunney outboxed Dempsey for the first six rounds, but in the seventh Dempsey finally connected with his mighty left hook and sent Tunney tumbling to the canvas. Referee Dave Barry started the count when Dempsey, instead of going to the farthest neutral corner, stood over Tunney, right fist cocked. After chasing Dempsey away, Barry began the count all over again. Tunney got up at nine after being down for fourteen seconds. He went on to completely control the fight, easily winning the ten rounds decision and ending Jack's career.

But the question remains, "How long was Tunney down? Could he have gotten up at the regular nine seconds?" So the Battle of the Long Count is still being debated today.

In much later years, Jack said, "Even new people come and assure me, I'm still champion and that I knocked Tunney out in the seventh round. It's nice of people to say so, but I'm not and I didn't." He said, "People refuse to believe Gene licked me when he did."

It was boxer with boxing ability, even with a scant amount of such ability, which gave him most trouble. Tunney whipped Dempsey twice with boxing ability and combined it with a sharp punch.

Jack retired after the second fight with Tunney. He had set a record for most first-round knockouts — twenty-four. He built his reputation with fists of steel on a line of victims, most of whom were never the same after Dempsey finished with them.

One of the knocks against Dempsey while he was champion was that he didn't fight the black fighter Harry Wills. Willis was the best fighter of his race and the top contender when Dempsey was champion.

Jack was criticized for not fighting Wills by the public. In response Jack said he was willing; whether he was or not didn't matter because the top promoter at that time, Tex Rickard, was against a Negro and a white to fight for the heavyweight title. The promoters never wanted another black champion like Jack Johnson.

After his fighting days, he became a man of many activities and a very restless individual, like in his fighting days. In New York he operated his popular and successful restaurant. He had been seen on television from the Stork Club and with Milton Berle, Jimmy Powers, and Ed Sullivan.

Jack still stayed active in boxing after retiring. He had been about everything a man can be in boxing: a fighter, promoter, manager, and referee. When Tex Rickard, the famous promoter, died in 1929, Dempsey jumped in and took over the promotion of the Jack Sharkey and Young Stribling fight in Miami Beach. In 1933 he promoted the Max Baer and Max Schmeling fight in New York. For publicity purposes he served as a sparring partner for both Baer and Schmeling. He also sold tickets for the fight. Later in 1935 he refereed the third Barney Boss and Jimmy McLarnin bout, and he managed Red Burman who fought Joe Louis for the title in 1941 and lost.

Demspey's effort to find a heavyweight fighter capable of winning the title had been hindered by his own great fighting ability. He wants his protégé to do the things he did. They couldn't. When he was fighting, he was one of the first big box-office draw. Before him there was no million-dollar gate. Jack was involved in four million dollar's gate fights.

With the success he had after his boxing days were over, he was an example of the good that can come from boxing if the individual has the ability, trains faithfully, and leads a clean life outside.

Gene Tunney

1. Tunney (rt) and Harry Greb square off just before start of 1922 bout, the only fight Gene ever lost. He beat Greb in later bouts.
2. Gene (rt) stopped Tom Gibbons in twelve, 1925.
3. Gene cleverly slips sparring partner's left.
4. Carpentier is kayoed by Tunney, July 1924.
5. Tunney shoots overhand hand right at Dempsey in winning title in Phila, 1926.
6. Dempsey dropped Gene in return match, but Tunney recovered to win.
7. In Gene's last fight before retirement, he stopped Tom Heeney (left), July 1928.

Gene Tunney

Born: 1897-1978, New York
Weight: 192 lbs, 6'
Champion: 1926-1928

Won: 77   Lost: 1   Drew: 3   Knockouts: 45

Gene Tunney is best remembered as the fighter who beat Jack Dempsey. He knew when to quit fighting and was the richest boxer who ever lived. What he really should be remembered for is that Tunney was an exceptionally brilliant strategist who planned each bout with infinite precision. Backing up his masterful strategy was Gene's boxing genius, his confidence, and his courage.

Tunney was strictly a scientific fighter who won most of his fights by wearing his opponents down. Even though Gene had forty-five knockouts, being the boxer in the ring was his style. Tunney was athletically inclined. He played baseball and basketball in high school. When he attended LaSalle Academy, he was on the varsity basketball team and later became a marathon runner.

From the time he first attended grammar school until he joined the marines in 1918, he sailed forth to conquer the world with his fists. At a very young age, he made up his mind to win the world heavyweight title. Growing up in New York, Tunney was always a fitness freak who wanted to have a good body. He would go to the athletic club when he was sixteen and box with both amateur and professional fighters.

Turning professionally in 1915 at the age of eighteen, Tunney fought as a light heavyweight. After winning his first twelve fights, he was drafted into the marine corps.

While in the marines, Gene did some boxing; he won the American Expeditionary Force championship as a light heavyweight, defeating Ted Jamieson in the finals. At the time Gene weighed only 166 pounds. After winning the light heavyweight, he defeated the heavyweight champion to have both.

Six months after getting out of the service, Billy Roche, a famous referee, took the young Tunney in hand. Under Roche, Gene won twenty-two contests in two years.

With this winning streak, he earned a title fight with Battling Levinsky for the American light heavyweight championship in 1922. Tunney startled the world when he won the title from Levinsky. Only then did he begin to gain some publicity.

Four months later Harry Greb relieved Gene of his title in a rough-and-tumble fight in the old Madison Square Garden. Incidentally, this was the first and only loss Tunney would ever have as a professional fighter. None of Gene's famous victories ever brought him the tribute he received the night he took that savage beating from Harry Greb.

Tunney never received much credit as a fighter. A lot of time mentioned the name Gene Tunney and most fans will think of backpedaling, and most fans will think rushes of Jack Dempsey after the long count fight. They would also say that Tunney was a fancy Dan who got to the top on a bicycle.

The people who saw the first Tunney and Harry Greb fight, when Gene bloodstained the canvas at the old Garden, knew nothing could be further from the truth. In this fight with Harry Greb on May 23, 1923, Tunney outweighed Greb 174 1/2 to 162 1/4. Tunny thought it was nothing to worry about.

The bell rang for round one; Tunney pranced out with his classical jabbing position. Greb tore in at him, gloves whirling red blades. Gene started a jab and bam! The first punch of the fight, a Greb left, exploded on Gene's nose, shattering the cartilage in two places. Greb stepped up the pace, burying Tunney under an avalanche of flying fists. Near the end of the round, more blood cascaded down Gene's face as Greb tore a four-inch cut over his left eye. The crowd sat in stunned amazement as Gene stood up under the merciless hammering and made it to the bell.

As the fight went on, Greb continued to pour on the pressure, slashing and raking Tunney with ripping combinations. Greb sliced open another cut over Gene's right eye, and by the eighth round, both fighters and the referee Kid McPartland were bathed in Gene's blood. But drawing from a secret well known only to champions, Gene fought back.

The same beating by Greb went on until the end of the fifteenth round. Gene kept trying, and he stayed on his feet. At the final bell, both his eyes were swollen shut, and his nose looked like a gigantic overripe plum. He was weak and wobbly and totally spent but still standing, and that took courage. The decision was a mere formality winner, a new light heavyweight champion of America, Harry Greb.

Tunney was half carried to his dressing room and the crowd nearly lifted the roof with its spontaneous tribute to a brave man. It was about the only night the people ever took Tunney to their hearts as one of their own.

Recalling the carnage in later years, Tunney said, "I had never bled so much before nor have I since. My seconds were unable to stop the bleeding over my eyes, one of which the left involved a severed artery, or that consequent to the nose fracture."

After losing his title in such a punishing way to Greb, many fighters may have wanted to hang it up because it may have taken their hearts out of the game. Not Gene, he wanted a rematch with Greb and got it.

The rematch was signed to fight on February 23, 1923. Tunney figured out the problems that he had in their first fight and went on and won a decisively fifteen rounds and his American light heavyweight title back from Greb.

Harry Greb now wanted a rematch to get the title back. Again Tunney beat Greb. Afterward Greb would say that Tunney would be the next heavyweight champion.

By 1924 Tunney had beaten the light heavyweight contenders. One of the light heavyweight contenders that he beat was former light heavyweight champion Georges Carpentier, who a couple of years earlier had fought and lost to the heavyweight champion Jack Dempsey.

In 1924 Tunney started fighting as a heavyweight. Previous to 1924 Tunney, because of his weight, was not regarded as a potential king of the heavyweights. He soon built his weight up to 190 pounds and more. With his extra weight, he now had muscles, bigger shoulders, and chest on a well-built frame. He still had the speed and footwork but had even more punching power.

Now fighting as a heavyweight in 1925, Gene knocked out Tommy Gibbons and Bartley Madden and defeated Johnny Risko. His knockout of Tommy Gibbons was big. Before this fight, Gibbons had never before been knocked down or out, and he was the man who had stayed fifteen rounds with the champion, Dempsey. After that win over Gibbons, it brought Tunney increased prestige. He became a marked man in the heavyweight division and he got a title fight with Jack Dempsey in 1926.

Gene got the chance to fight Jack Dempsey on September 23, 1926. From the beginning Dempsey made his fiercest rushes, but Tunney's counters offset them. His boxing ability was too much for Dempsey. Only in the fourth round did Dempsey threaten. It was evident midway through the fight that Dempsey had to score a knockout to win. Dempsey was marked for Tunney's jarring left and heavy-handed right crosses that tired the champion out. Being a big underdog, Tunney got an easy decision and the title.

What surprised a lot of people in the Tunney and Dempsey fight was Tunney's ability to rough it up on close quarter with the powerful-hitting Dempsey and to be able to take control by tying up Dempsey.

After beating Dempsey, Tunney was an unpopular champion. The public never accepted him because he defeated their hero and because he was not a hard-nosed fighter like Dempsey. After winning the title, his first defense was a rematch with Dempsey in 1927.

The rematch with Dempsey was mostly the same as the first. Dempsey was taking the aggressive in the fight with Tunney. Tunney was countering with straight left jabs and always blocking carefully. Tunney piled up points by using his left jab and some short rights to the head. Tunney had the legs to keep moving round after round. Dempsey didn't have the legs as his rushed attacks got less vicious.

Dempsey's only chance came in the seventh round when he knocked Tunney down with a left hook. Tunney got fourteen seconds to get up because Dempsey wouldn't go to a neutral corner. When Tunney did get up, his legs were still good as he backpedaled away from Dempsey's attacks the rest of the round using the entire ring.

After the seventh round, Tunney's head was clear, and he went back to jabbing. Dempsey had gashes over both eyes, cut lip, and puffed mouth. He was a beaten fighter, and Tunney won a unanimous decision. The fight would go down in history as the Battle of the Long Count.

Tunney had his last fight on July 26, 1928, when he fought Tom Heeney. He won this fight in the eleventh round on a TKO when the referee stopped it because Heeney was helpless at the time to the scientific Tunney who was able to do anything he wanted to do to Heeney.

After the win over Heeney, Tunney retired the same year in 1928. He was to the point, and nothing could temp him not to retire or make a comeback, even though promoters tried. He had already made a fortune in the ring. His two fights with Jack Dempsey were all-time-record, million-dollar gate fights. At this time in Tunney's career, he probably was in his prime, and no fighter could beat him.

In the process of achieving his goal, Tunney had fought eighty-one times with only one loss — that, as a light heavyweight early in his career. Every fight was thoroughly planned. When his fighting days were over, Tunney got married and became a highly successful millionaire. He wasn't one of the fighters who spent their money unwisely when fighting, only to end up broke after their career was over.

Not fighting now, Tunney became a very smart businessman. He owned his own construction company, was on the board of directors of several large corporations, and was the commander of his American Legion Post. In World War II, he became a captain in the navy and was in charge of the physical training program.

In the years Tunney was champion, he was underrated by the boxing fans because he succeeded a popular titleholder in Jack Dempsey. As years went by, Tunney received his due for his fine fighting qualities as one of the truly great heavyweight champions.

Title Vacant: August 1, 1928-June 12, 1930

The second title vacant happened in 1928 when Gene Tunney retired as the world champion. An elimination tournament was set up with the top four contenders to fight for the vacant title.

The four top fighters were Max Schmeling, Paulino Uzcudun, Phil Scott, and Jack Sharkey. After almost two years without a world heavyweight champion, Max Schmeling won the tournament to become the new heavyweight champion of the world in 1930.

Max Schmeling

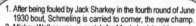

1. After being fouled by Jack Sharkey in the fourth round of June 1930 bout, Schmeling is carried to corner, the new champ.
2. Mickey Walker was no match for Max's bruising blows.
3. After losing decision—and title—to Sharkey in return bout, Max leaves ring in seeming disbelief that he lost.
4. Steve Hamas (left) won upset decision over Max but was brutally beaten by Max in return bout in Germany, 1935.
5. The startling knockout of Joe Louis by Schmeling in 1936
6. After kayoing Louis, Schmeling acknowledges cheers from crowd. Except for closed left eye, he was unmarked.
7. Today Schmeling is a very successful business man in Hanburg and acclaimed best German athlete in history.

Max Schmeling

Born: 1905-2005, Germany
Weight: 190 lbs., 6'1"
Champion: 1930-1932

Won: 56   Lost: 10   Drew: 4   Knockouts: 38

The name Max Schmeling brings back the memory of two fights that will always be remembered in heavyweight boxing history. One is, he is the only man ever to win the heavyweight title on a foul and for his sensational kayo of Joe Louis in 1936.

Schmeling was always in shape for his fights, strong, and determined, with a kayo right fist. When he fought he didn't take the risks, preferring instead to bide his time and wait for the big opening.

Born in Germany in 1905, growing up he was required to fight and exercise for war daily. At sixteen he traveled throughout Europe doing different jobs. Max got his first chance in the ring as a sparring partner for a professional fighter. After that he was determined to be a fighter in the ring.

Starting his career in 1924, Schmeling fought as a middleweight at the age of nineteen. He didn't have much trouble his first year with nine victories in ten fights.

Fighting in Germany, he beat all of the German top fighters. At the age of twenty-two, Max won the European light heavyweight title. At twenty-three he was the German heavyweight champion and gradually got the reputation as a knockout puncher.

Schmeling continued to fight in Germany until 1928. He decided to go to the United States in 1928 to have bigger fights and more money. This was also the same year Gene Tunney retired as heavyweight champion.

After being in the United States that year in 1928, Max had his first fight in the United States against Joe Monte, whom he knocked out. The win over Monte got him some attention as a good new fighter.

When Schmeling first came to America, an important part of his publicity campaign was built around his strong facial resemblance to Jack Dempsey.

In 1929 the name Max Schmeling was a household name to all boxing people. This was mainly because he knocked out Johnny Risko in nine rounds. Risko was a contender to the title and also had gone the distance with Gene Tunney.

Max won his first five fights after getting to the States. In less than a year, he had made a name for himself and was one of the top contenders to the vacant title.

At this time in 1929, it was said that Schmeling, Jack Sharkey, and Paulino Uzcudun were said to be the best contenders to find a new champion.

It was set up for Schmeling and Uzcudun to fight each other on June 27, 1929, and the winner to fight Sharky to find the new champion. Schmeling won a unanimous decision over Uzcudun setting the stage to fight Sharkey for the title.

Schmeling and Jack Sharkey fought on June 12, 1930. Schmeling won the fight and the title on a foul in the fourth round. In the round Schmeling was hit low and hard by a left from Sharkey. Max fell to the floor clutching his groin. Going into the fourth round, Sharkey was winning the fight, and Schmeling was still an active fighter.

The referee Jim Crowley was confused of what had happened and tried to get some help from the two judges. Neither of the judges had seen the quick left punch by Sharkey.

Schmeling's cornermen picked him up off the canvas and carried him to his corner. Crowley had to make a quick decision on his own. His decision was for Max to have a brief rest period and then continue to fight. His manager said he couldn't fight and should get the title on a foul. So Crowley ended up disqualifying Sharkey and named Schmeling the new heavyweight champion of the world. It was the only time a champion had won a fight lying on the canvas. Later in the dressing room, Max's manager showed the cup Max was wearing and the dent in the cup to justify the decision.

The American people weren't too impressed with the new champion because of the way he won the title. Back in Germany he was a hero. When he beat Sharkey for the title, he became the first German fighter to win the title and the first foreigner since Bob Fitzsimmons to win the title over thirty years ago.

The boxing people wanted a quick rematch between Schmeling and Sharkey to settle the dispute of their first fight. The problem was Schmeling's camp wasn't in any quick hurry to sign to fight Sharkey.

From the time Schmeling came to the United States to fight, his manager was Joe Jacobs. He got him fights real early, early ranking; Schmeling did good, and Jacobs was real good for Schmeling as his manager. Jacobs wanted Sharkey later after Schmeling made some money from fighting other contenders. Jacobs also knew that to make the big money, the champion had to pick his fights for as long as he could.

Schmeling left the states after winning the title and stayed in Germany over a year. He came back to the States to defend his title. Instead of fighting Sharkey, they signed to fight young Willie Stribling on July 3, 1931.

Jacobs knew that a fight with Jack Sharkey was a bigger risk; Stribling was less of a risk. He also knew that a return fight with Sharkey was going to happen, anyway, but he could make some money with this title fight with Stribling then.

In the fight with Willie Stribling, it went the way Jacob had thought it would go. Schmeling punish Stribling for fifteen rounds until the referee stopped it in the fifteenth round.

Schmeling went back to Germany for another year. He came back to fight a return fight with Jack Sharkey on June 31, 1932. Two years had passed since their first fight. After how he had won the championship from Sharkey in 1930, Schmeling wanted to win this fight with Sharkey bad to prove to the public that he could beat Sharkey.

The fight against Sharkey for the title went fifteen rounds, and everybody at the fight — the fans, the crowd, and Schmeling's corner — figured Schmeling had built up enough points to have a safe lead to win. The crowd was shocked when the announcer said Jack Sharkey was the winner and new heavyweight champion.

Schmeling said he was robbed, and his manager Jacobs ran around the ring saying we were robbed. Even the fifteenth and final round, everybody thought that Schmeling had won. This is one of the most controversial fights of all times; the boxing commission was forced to investigate, but Schmeling wound up the ex-champion of the world.

Because Schmeling was from Germany and because Adolf Hitler was their leader, Schmeling was often booed before and in his fights. Because of his great showing in defeat and the verdict, this was his most popular fight in win or defeat.

Losing his title the way he did, Schmeling wanted a third fight with Sharkey to get the title back. But after he lost his title in 1932, he was an up-and-down fighter.

In 1933 Schmeling lost two fights. One was a fight with Max Baer where Baer's powerful right finished Schmeling by knocking him out in ten rounds. The other was a loss to Steve Hamas. After these two losses, Max went back to Germany to fight. He then returned to the United States to make another run at the title.

Then Schmeling started winning his fights, working his way up to getting a chance to fight the up-and-coming Joe Louis. Three years after losing his title, Schmeling pulled off one of the biggest upsets in heavyweight history, a win over a young Joe Louis in 1936. He was a 10-1 underdog to the undefeated 27-0 Louis, who had destroyed all of his previous opponents.

Before the fight with Louis, Max had said he had seen a weakness in Louis's style of fighting. What the weakness that Max saw was that he could use his right hand after Louis had thrown a left because Louis dropped his left after he threw a left.

In the Schmeling and Louis fight, the plan worked perfectly. Max fought mostly as a counterpuncher. Every time Louis would throw a jab, he would drop his left, and Max just kept shooting his right hand over it with a powerful right to the head. His right hand worked good enough to put Louis down in the fourth, knocking Louis out in the twelfth round. Everybody who saw the fight at that time was surprised to see that Schmeling, and not Louis, was landing the knockout punches.

With his knockout win over Joe Louis, Max became a top contender for the title again. And after his great win over Louis, Adolph Hitler became his top fan. Hitler treated him like a king as he was trying to take over the world, using Schmeling's great win over Louis as a symbol of German power. Even though all this was laid on him, he really just considered himself a fighter and not a politician.

Schmeling wanted badly to fight the current champion James Braddock for the title after his win over Louis. But he didn't get to fight Braddock for the title. For one reason because it was feared that Schmeling may win the title and keep it in Germany. Then there was the smart promoter Mike Jacobs who represented Joe Louis and who convinced Braddock to fight Louis instead of Schmeling.

Joe Louis went on and won the title from Jim Braddock. With Louis now the champion, Schmeling set his eyes on now winning the title from Louis. Louis agreed to the fight, mostly to get a fight to get back at Schmeling for beating him in their first fight in 1936. The fight wasn't a fight as Louis pounded Schmeling for the short time it lasted in winning in the first round.

This would be Max's last fight in the United States. He went back to Germany to end his boxing career overseas where he fought until he was forty-three years old, when he lost a ten-round decision to Richard Vogt in Germany in 1948.

When his career in boxing was over, he became a very successful businessman and a millionaire. Schmeling was acclaimed the best German athlete in history.

Jack Sharkey

1. Sharkey (left) gave Harry Wills a bad beating before Wills fouled out in thirteenth.
2. Jack (right) training for Dempsey bout in 1927
3. Dempsey's hook knocked out Sharkey in round seven.
4. Young Stribling (rt) lost decision to Jack, 1929.
5. Referee disallowed Phil Scott's foul claim and awarded Miami bout to Sharkey on TKO, 1930.
6. Sharkey's kayo of Tommy Loughran (left) was a big upset. But Tommy later decisioned Jack.
7. Today Sharkey lives an easy life, occasionally referees major bouts, such as Archie Moore vs. Yvon Durelle. Here Jack counts out Durelle.

Jack Sharkey

Born: 1902-1994, New York
Weight: 205 lbs., 6′
Champion: 1932-1933

Won: 38   Lost: 14   Drew: 3   Knockouts: 14

Jack Sharkey was one of the most underrated heavyweight champions of all. He had superb boxing skills and jolting punching power and was fast and a good boxer.

As a fighter he was probably in more controversial fights than any other champion. Sharkey had natural talent that was sometimes overshadowed by his erraticism and eccentricities. This behavior hurt Sharkey's career that might have been better than what it was. His career was colorful and crowded with controversy from beginning to end.

Jack went into the navy in 1920. This is when he started getting into boxing, mostly because of his well-conditioned body. He served three and a half years in the service.

The whole time he was fighting in the navy, he never had a teacher, just his natural ability. Still doing his service years, he lost only one fight. Getting out of the service in 1924, Jack turned to boxing full time and turned pro the same year.

Born Joseph Paul Cukoschay on October 6, 1902, he took the name Jack Sharkey from a former boxing idol of his, named Tom Sharkey.

His first couple of years, he was an unknown fighter. Then Sharkey beat Eddie Huffman in 1926, and boxing people began to be aware of his ability. By the late 1920s, Sharkey was as well known as any top contender, mostly by beating top fighters like Johnny Risko and Harry Wills.

The win over Harry Wills in 1926 got Sharkey the fame he needed. He beat the feared black fighter Wills in thirteen rounds.

People still haven't forgotten that the great Jack Dempsey wouldn't fight Wills. This win over Wills got Sharkey more money, better fights, and made him a contender to the title.

The win over Harry Wills got Sharkey in an elimination tournament held in Madison Square Garden in 1927 to determine the champion Gene Tunney's next challenger. Jack eliminated Mike McTigue with 14,181 looking on and box office reporting receipts of $132,147.

The winner between Jim Maloney and Jack Delaney was won by Maloney, pitting him against Sharkey. The winners Sharkey and Maloney had moved to the outdoor Yankee Stadium for the next episode in the series; and a crowd of 24,058 contributed $232,199 to see Sharkey turn in a sensational five-round knockout over Maloney.

The grand final of the eliminations had pitted Sharkey against Jack Dempsey. This fight was also in the stadium; and 72,283 payees accounted for a gross of $1,083, 529, which is a record for a nonchampionship bout.

Sharkey and Dempsey fought on July 21, 1927. Sharkey had Dempsey badly battered in the early rounds, boxing superbly. Fighting as a boxer, Sharkey used his speed and fought outside from Dempsey's power. Then he started going inside when Dempsey started pounding him mostly to the body.

In the seventh round, Sharkey's fiery temper cost him. In the round Dempsey landed a blow that Sharkey thought was low. He then turned his head away from his opponent and toward the referee to complain of a low blow, where then Dempsey landed a hook to the jaw that knocked out Sharkey.

Instead of Sharkey, Dempsey qualified for a return fight with Gene Tunney, causing Sharkey to miss his first shot at a title fight. After losing to Dempsey, he would lose one more fight to Johnny Risko and then win eight fights in a year. These fights would put him in the top search to find a champion after Gene Tunney had retired as champion.

Sharkey had to fight Phil Scott, the English heavyweight champion, on February 27, 1930, with the winner to meet Max Schmeling for the championship fight. Jack won the fight with Scott in three rounds setting the stage to fight Schmeling for the title.

On June 12, 1930, Jack was pitted against Max Schmeling to find a new heavyweight champion. The title had been vacant since Gene Tunney retired in 1928.

This was Sharkey's first title fight. In this fight Sharkey won the first three rounds easily. Then in the fourth round, a wild left by him got away and hit Schmeling low. Sharkey was disqualified and lost his first chance to become champion. This was another controversial fight that Sharkey was in.

Jack was eager to get Schmeling in the ring again, but he had to wait. After Schmeling won the title, he went to Germany for a year only to come back to the States and fight young Willie Stribling and not him. Schmeling again went back to Germany for another year.

While waiting to get a rematch with Schmeling, he fought Mickey Walker, a middleweight, to a fifteen-round draw. Jack then won fifteen rounds over Primo Carnera, a top fighter.

Schmeling and Sharkey finally met on June 21, 1932. Jack was a 6-5 favorite. They fought fifteen rounds, and Sharkey got a very controversial decision. Most people thought he had lost.

In Sharkey's first title defense, he fought Primo Carnera on June 29, 1933. Going into the fight, boxing fans believed that Sharkey was much superior to Carnera. Sharkey won three of the first four rounds easily. Then in the sixth round, it was a right to the chin, and it was over. Sharkey was down, out, and motionless.

When he lost his title to Carnera, it was a surprise to everyone, especially because he had previously beaten Carnera with ease.

After his title was gone, he lost his next two fights. One loss was to King Levinsky, and the other was to Tommy Loughran. He then retired.

He made a comeback on August 15, 1936, fighting Joe Louis. Jack was now on the comeback trail. You could see that he was way past his prime. He was coming out of retirement hoping a win over Louis would put him back in the heavyweight race.

At the time of the fight, Sharkey was twelve years older. Louis put Jack down in the second and three times in the third to win by a knockout.

One of the reasons why Sharkey was underrated as a champion was his lack of self-control, which overshadowed his superb boxing skills. When he got mad, he changed instantly from master boxer to brawler.

After leaving the ring, Sharkey lived the easy life, occasionally refereeing major bouts and fishing in New Hampshire.

Primo Carnero

1. Primo and his discoverer Leon See in Paris, 1928
2. Publicity photo taken in London park, 1929
3. Ernie Schaaf slumps to floor after taking jab.
4. Weighing in for title-winning bout with Jack Sharkey in 1933, Primo scored six-round kayo.
5. Carnera made successful title defense against much smaller Tommy Loughran at Miami, 1934.
6. Primo wrestled professionally in the 1940s and 1950s. People were still curious about the famous giant, and big crowds always turned out for his matches. He settled in California but returned to his native Italy to die.

Primo Carnera

Born: 1906-1967, Italy
Weight: 260 lbs., 6'5¾
Champion: 1933-1934

Won: 88   Lost: 14   Drew: 0   Knockouts: 69

Primo Carnera was the heaviest man to hold the world heavyweight title. He was probably the best built and strongest of all of the champions. He also was one of the least skillful of all the champions.

Some of the things said about Carnera's boxing skills were an unjust appraisal because he wasn't all that bad. As a fighter he had a very good jab; his hands were fast; he moved around the ring well for a man his size, and he had courage to match his size.

When boxing people said that Primo didn't have much skill in the ring, it had a lot to do with him being clumsy at times in the ring. This is where his size may have held him back somewhat. By him being a big muscle-bound man, his body probably was made more for weight lifting than boxing. Primo didn't have the agility as the smaller fighters had.

With all the strength he possessed, he never had what you call punching power. Although Primo had sixty-nine knockouts, he was a light hitter.

Carnera's two biggest downfalls in the ring were, he didn't have what all fighters needed: some of both the killer instinct and a hard chin. He was too nice. He never wanted to hurt anybody, and he couldn't take a punch.

Born in Italy October 25, 1906, he left home at fourteen to go to France. While in France at the age of sixteen, he joined a traveling circus as a strongman and as a wrestler. It was at the circus in 1928 that he got discovered by Paul Journee, mainly because of Carnera's size. Journee figured with his size, he could become a boxer. Journee got Leon See to manage Carnera, teaching him how to box.

Carnera had his first fight in the same year in 1928. As expected he was clumsy but powerful and too strong for his opponent that he won by a knockout in two rounds.

He stayed in France for a while where he got some more knockouts, and then started to travel out of France to fight. He traveled all over the continent. The promoters wanted to show off this big, huge fighter. Fighting overseas he won seventeen of his first eighteen fights.

Carnera came to the United States to fight in 1929. He ran up a lot of victories. These were just average fighters he fought. He had a total of twenty-four fights and lost only one. This was a ten-round-decision loss to Jim Maloney.

Primo then left to go back and fight overseas. He came back to fight in the States in 1931. His first fight was a rematch against Jim Maloney. This time he got revenge and won a ten-round decision over Maloney.

Now back in the States, he ran off another string of victories, but not against top fighters. He soon was pitted against the top contender to the title, Jack Sharkey. He lost to the more experience Sharkey but figured he was ready for the top contenders.

Carnera then defeated King Levinsky, a very good fighter, to let people know that he could beat good fighters. In a rematch with Levinsky, he again defeated Levinsky.

On February 10, 1933, Carnera fought Ernie Schaaf. This was a very important fight for Carnera and Schaaf. Jack Sharkey, the new champion, had said he would be willing to defend his title against the winner of the fight. The fight went thirteen rounds when Carnera landed a light punch and Schaaf went down and out. The people thought that it was fake because Schaaf had done almost nothing through the fight.

Ernie Schaaf died in a hospital three days later. It had become known later that Schaaf had never fully recovered from head injuries suffered in a bout with Max Baer a year before. The death of Ernie Schaaf had a profound effect on Primo, and it is doubtful if he ever threw a punch with full power after he saw Schaaf carried from the ring.

After the death of Schaaf, Carnera was exonerated. Bill Muldoon, chairman of the New York State Athletic Commission, announced that Primo Carnera would be barred from fighting Jack Sharkey for the title because he was too big and dangerous for average heavyweight to fight. Carnera would have to fight in a special division for bigger heavyweights like him.

Bill Muldoon later changed his mind and let Carnera fight Jack Sharkey for the title on June 29, 1933. Carnera won this fight over Sharkey and the title on a one-punch knockout in the sixth round.

While being champion, Carnera had two successful defenses of the title. He beat Paulino Uzcudun on October 22, 1933, by a fifteen-round decision; and on March 1, 1934, he defeated Tommy Loughran also on a fifteen-round decision.

His third defense was against Max Baer on June 14, 1934. This was a wild fight. Carnera was floored eleven times before it was halted in the eleventh round. Sometime both fighters went to the floor at the same time. Carnera won some of the middle rounds but was unable to avoid Baer's powerful right thrown in the fight.

With his title now gone, Carnera's boxing career went down. One year after losing his title, he was knocked out by Joe Louis in the sixth round. He was knocked out by Leroy Haynes in three rounds, and in the rematch he was knocked out by Haynes in the ninth round.

When Carnera was fighting, he never received a fair share of his earning; because of his good nature, he was used by the mob and other people. The mob only wanted him for the money he could make them. He hardly ever had money, friends, or family. Many of the boxing people believe that Carnera was involved in a lot of fixed fights.

After losing his title and not having money, he continued to fight, winning some against no-name fighters. It got so bad for him that he couldn't get a fight.

Still needing money, Carnera changed his sport to professional wrestling. He was a wrestler in the 1940s and 1950s. Because he was Primo Carnera, the former world heavyweight boxing champion of the world, he did real well as a wrestler. Every week

that he wrestled, he drew sellout crowds. He was a crowd-pleaser
He now had money that the mob didn't take.

He continued to live in the United States and bought a house.
He stayed in the States till he got sick. He went back home to Italy
in 1967 to die on his home soil.

Max Baer

1. Baer (left) was beaten by Ernie Schaaf in 1930 but upset Ernie in 1932 return match.
2. Schmeling (rt) is protected by referee after being stopped by Baer in tenth round, 1933.
3. Max, his father, Jacob, and brother Buddy
4. Max kayoed Carnera in eleventh to win title, 1934.
5. Baer after being stopped by Lou Nova (rt), 1941
6. Max did something not even Joe Louis could do—knock down tough Tommy Farr. Baer won.
7. Max had enough left to stop Tony Galento, 1940.
8. Last picture of Baer taken shortly before he died of a heart attack in Hollywood, 1959

Max Baer

Born: 1909-1959, Nebraska
Weight: 209 lbs., 6'2"
Champion: 1934-1935

Won: 70   Lost: 13   Drew: 0   Knockouts: 52

Max Baer was a showman, a glamour boy with a tremendous public following. He appeared to the public as very lovable.

As a fighter he had it all to be the best. He was a good puncher, killing power in his right hand, and had a great physical body. Baer had all the physical requirements and probably could have been a great champion.

With all he had going for him, the thing that held him up that all fighters needed he didn't have, dedication and a mental aspect of what he had. What Max loved was being the showman, the clown in the ring, having fun and delighting the fans with his clowning.

Max had a mighty right hand and knew it. He enjoyed knocking people out. Max would, in a match, tell an opponent he would trade three of their punches for one of his and mean it.

At the age of sixteen, Max was an expert butcher and cattle killer, swinging an ax with plenty of power, working for his father in his butchering business, living in Livermore, California. Baer would say in later years that he attributed the tremendous force of his punch to the powerful muscles he had developed wielding a meat ax.

Max got interested in boxing after he got into a fight at a dance with a locomotive engineer. Max landed one punch, a right, and it landed flush on the jaw, and the engineer was out. At the time Max was a husky eighteen years of age, six feet tall, and weighed 190 pounds. That one-punch fight gave Max ideas. He soon bought a punching bag and gloves and set up a small gym on his father's ranch. Soon the people around him convinced Max he should be a boxer in the ring.

Baer started fighting professionally in 1929 at the age of twenty. His first pro fight was against Chief Caribou whom he knocked out. His first year of fighting was a busy year. Most of his wins were knockouts. Being the first year, the competition wasn't that great.

At this time in his career, Baer was fighting mostly in Oakland and San Francisco. He started to fight stiffer opponents and still had good success. He soon became one of the outstanding box-office draws on the Pacific coast.

In his second year of fighting, he fought a fighter named Frankie Campbell, the fight paid Baer ten thousand dollars. In the fifth round of a furious fight, Baer knocked Campbell out. What was sad about the fight was that Campbell never regained consciousness. Max was deeply hurt by the outcome of the fight and though about retiring from the ring. His people managed to get Baer to leave the West Coast and go east to fight and get away from the depression of the Campbell fight. He had his first fight in Madison Square Garden on December 19, 1930. He fought Ernie Schaaf who was too experienced and beat Baer by a ten-round decision.

In January 1931, he defeated Tom Heeney in three rounds. It was the same Heeney who had fought Gene Tunney for the title and lost.

Between fights Baer would lose three fights. One was to Tommy Loughran, a real smart fighter, and a ten-round-decision loss to Johnny Risko.

The last one was a fight promoted by Jack Dempsey for twenty rounds with Paulino Uzcudun. Uzcudun got the decision. After this loss Baer wouldn't lose another fight for four years.

He got a rematch with Johnny Risko and beat him soundly. Max then beat the dangerous King Levinsky by a decision on January 29, 1932. Then on August 31, 1932, he got a rematch with Ernie Schaaf, who had beaten him earlier.

Baer now was a better fighter than he was the first time, but Schaaf was good too. The fight was very even. In the tenth round, Baer staggered Schaaf with three thunderous rights and chased him around the ring with a vicious attack of the face and body.

Two seconds before the bell rang, in the end of the fight, Schaff collapsed from the punishment. Several minutes passed before Schaaf was revived sufficiently to leave the ring. It was the terrific beating he absorbed in this battle that was believed to be the real cause of Schaaf's tragic death, which took place not six months in his bout with Primo Carnera.

By now Baer was a contender for the title. Before this could happen, he was to fight the former champion Max Schmeling on June 8, 1933.

Schmeling did most of the leading in the fight, fighting steady and winning on points late in the fight. Baer was doing everything to get into the fight, swarming all over Schmeling and even using dirty tactics that he was repeatedly warned of.

In the ninth round, Baer tore into Schmeling with everything. Some were blocked, and some were countered by Schmeling, but the ones that got through hurt Schmeling a lot.

When the tenth round started, it was more of the same with Baer pressing the action. In the round Baer threw a hard right that staggered Schmeling on the ropes. At this point Schmeling was badly hurt, then Baer landed another right landing on Schmeling's chin that knocked him down. At nine he was up but weak. Baer was all over him again until the referee Arthur Donovan stopped the fight. This win made Baer the top contender to the title.

A year would go by before he would fight Primo Carnera for the title on June 14, 1934.

Going into the fight with Carnera, Baer was the underdog. Even though Baer weighed 210 pounds, he was said to be too small for the big strong Carnera. The Carnera and Baer fight was one of the weirdest championship matches in the history of heavyweight fights.

The bout had a strange blend of exciting drama and comedy of clever boxing, mauling, and wrestling. From the start of the fight, the boxing world misjudged Baer's hard-hitting right hand. In the first round alone, he knocked Carnera down three times.

Baer landed terrific punches when he wasn't clowning. Carnera had a lot of courage that was wasted by clumsiness. Carnera was knocked down eleven times and on several other occasions fell down. Referee Arthur Donovan finally stopped it in the eleventh round with Carnera helpless.

Even though the fight with Carnera was his first championship fight, Baer was still clowning in the fight. As champion, Baer kept busy by boxing exhibitions, night clubs, and radio performances.

Baer's first defense of the title came a year after he won it. It was against James Braddock on June 13, 1935. Max was a huge favorite to win the fight, a 10-1 favorite. He didn't take the fight seriously, saying he would knock Braddock out inside of six rounds.

Baer didn't even train properly for the title fight. He paid for it in the fight as he fought listlessly most of the fight. He was in poor condition and tired by the eighth round. His punches didn't have the normal power in it. All the time Braddock was much too fast for Baer. He fought a smart fight of boxing and jabbing, in winning a unanimous decision and the title over Baer.

Again being in a championship fight, he was clowning in the ring. This time he wasn't as lucky to get away with it as he was when he beat Primo Carnera for the title.

Baer then signed to fight the up-and-coming Joe Louis on September 24, 1935, to get back into contention for the title. This time he trained hard but was still disappointing, and Louis pounded him into submission in four rounds.

On April 15, 1937, Baer fought the British heavyweight champion Tommy Farr and was beaten in twelve rounds. They had a rematch on March 11, 1938. This time Baer gave Farr a sound whipping to win in fifteen rounds. Max now had high hopes on getting a rematch with the now champion Joe Louis.

After the Farr fight, his career was winning and losing. One of his better fights was when he fought Tony Galento on July 2, 1940. He completely battered Galento into submission in eight rounds.

Two of Baer's setbacks were against Lou Nova. On June 1, 1939, Nova stopped Baer in the eleventh round. In the rematch on April 4, 1941, Nova knocked Baer out in the eighth round. With this loss, he was no longer a contender, and he retired after the Nova fight.

With his boxing days over, Baer was a physical training instructor for the army air force during World War II. After his time in the service, he turned to stage and became a popular attraction in theaters and night clubs.

Baer loved life. He loved to laugh and spend money. Experts in boxing will always debate how great a fighter Max would have been if he had devoted as much time to training as he did to enjoying himself. Baer wouldn't have wanted it any other way. Being the beloved clown was a lot more fun than being champion.

James Braddock

1. Braddock (rt) lost a decision to Leo Lomski, 1929.
2. Jimmy (rt) tried for Tommy Loughran's light heavyweight title in 1929, but was beaten.
3. Jim scored upset of century by winning heavyweight title from Max Baer on June 13, 1935
4. Braddock (left) was thirty when he beat Baer, four years older than Max. But Jim was much faster.
5. Jim trains for title defense against Joe Louis.
6. In his last fight, Braddock defeated Tommy Farr in New York on January 21, 1938.
7. With Gus Lesnevich (left), boxing's goodwill ambassador Braddock ballyhoos Carmen Basilio.

James "Jim" Braddock

Born: 1906-1974, New York
Weight: 197 lbs., 6'3"
Champion: 1935-1937

Won: 51   Lost: 25   Drew: 6   Knockouts: 26

Jim Braddock had an unbelievable career of determination and courage. Coming all the way from public relief to being heavyweight champion of the world, he was called the Cinderella Man because of his rags-to-riches. In the ring he was a good boxer and puncher and had a lot of courage.

At an early age living in New Jersey, Braddock got into a lot of fights at school and showed natural fighting ability. He soon was encouraged to try amateur boxing.

Braddock had a good teacher early in his career in his brother Joe Braddock, who was a prizefighter. With his brother Joe teaching him, Jim was the New Jersey amateur light heavyweight champion in 1925 and 1926.

Doing good as an amateur but not making money, Braddock decided to turn pro in 1926 at the age of twenty-one. He got Joe Gould to be his manager. Braddock was fighting as a light heavyweight, which he fought a number of years as.

With Gould as his manager in his first year in 1926, Braddock was very successful. Against not-too-strong opponents, he was undefeated in fifteen fights with eleven knockouts.

In 1927, Braddock had seventeen fights with only one defeat. This was a lost to an experienced fighter named Paul Cavalier. These were tougher opponents than he had his first year.

Braddock started making a name for himself when he beat Pete Lateo in ten rounds. Then he knocked out Tuffy Griffith, a fighter that everybody was talking big about, in two rounds. He was the underdog in both of the fights that he won. The young

119

Braddock was being talked into fighting for the light heavyweight title.

Starting 1929 he lost a decision to Leo Lomski. Then Braddock knocked out a good fighter in Jim Slattery in nine rounds. In winning the match with Slattery, he earned a shot at the light-heavyweight title held by Tommy Loughran.

Loughran and Braddock fought on June 18, 1929. Loughran was too good, smart, and clever a fighter for Braddock to win an easy fifteen-round decision.

Braddock couldn't win the light-heavyweight title but was able to win the tougher heavyweight title later in his career; glory and money came later for him.

Before fighting Loughran for the title, Braddock seemed like he was going to have a good career, but the loss for the title took some of the fire out of Braddock. In the next three years of fighting, he would lose thirteen fights. Fighting as a light heavyweight, Braddock was an unsuccessful contender. A lot of these losses were against good fighters like Maxie Rosenbloom and Ernie Schaaf.

Then in 1933, it was more of the same—win some and lose some. Braddock was written off as a washed-up fighter. Doing so bad in the ring, he couldn't convince the promoters that he was worth another chance. He was broke with a wife and three kids. He retired from the ring the same year being unsatisfied with his boxing career.

At the time he retired from the ring, the depression was going on. He spent what little bit that he had saved up from boxing on his family of four. He tried getting a job on the dock, but it wasn't enough for his family. In just a short time, he was flat broke. He had to seek help from the New Jersey Welfare Board.

Nine months would go by being out of the ring. Braddock was then approached about fighting Corn Griffin. Jim jumped at the thought of getting back into the ring. With three children to feed, no job, and needing the money the way he did, he had to fight. He made the comeback that carried him to the championship and immortality.

Jim was now on the comeback trail and was considered as a tune-up fighter for contender. For his first comeback fight against Corn Griffin, he was considered as a stepping stone for Griffin.

Corn Griffin was a rising young heavyweight — speedy, clever, and had made a name for himself. Jim trained hard for this fight and got in the best shape he could.

In the very first round, Griffin was all over Braddock and knocked him down. The second round was different as Braddock started punching and landing a right that ended the fight. This contest brought him into the spotlight.

Three months later Jim was signed to fight John Henry Lewis. Lewis was a contender. He had beaten Braddock two years earlier. Lewis was the favorite because they thought he was too fast for the slow Braddock.

As in the Corn Griffin fight, Braddock came through again. Knocking Lewis down in the seventh round, he went on and won a ten-round decision.

Now Braddock was back in the thick of things. He was soon signed to fight Art Lasky on March 22, 1935. This was a very important fight for Braddock. Max Baer, the champion, was supposed to fight Art Lasky after Lasky first beat Braddock.

Jim fought a very smart fight and landed accurate punches in leading on points all the way. At the end of fifteen rounds, he had won a unanimous decision. Instead of Lasky it was Braddock who fought Max Baer for the title on June 13, 1935.

In the title fight against Baer, Braddock was a big 10-1 underdog to win. Never in heavyweight history has a challenger been given less of a chance to win was Braddock.

In the fight Braddock fought a smart fight by not trading punches with the hard-hitting Baer. Instead he outboxed and outfoxed Baer and used his left jab and piled up points. Baer couldn't score any of his haymaker because Braddock either blocked them or ducked from them. Braddock got the decision and the title.

In just one year, he had come from receiving public assistance, and not knowing from where his next meal would come to being the heavyweight champion of the world.

For the next two years, Braddock didn't defend his title. He toured the country, boxing and refereeing exhibitions and doing stage and radio appearances.

Now it was past time for Braddock to fight somebody. Max Schmeling was still around, and the young Joe Louis was a top contender. Jim decided to go with Joe Louis for his first defense of the title.

Braddock and Louis fought on June 22, 1937. Now at the age of thirty-one, out of the ring for two years, he was no longer the same fighter who beat Max Baer for the title. He was now ring rusty going up against the feared Joe Louis.

Braddock fought his heart out against Louis in the bout, even knocking Joe down in the first round from a short right to the chin. After the first round, it was all Louis. He was too young, too strong, and too vicious a puncher for Braddock. By the fifth round, Braddock's thirty-one years of age was beginning to show, but Braddock kept fighting. Coming out in the eighth round, his legs was gone and his arms heavy; Louis had no problem nailing him with a hard right and knocking him out to become the new champion.

Seven months later, it was Braddock against Tommy Farr on January 21, 1938. Just before the fight, Farr had gone fifteen rounds with the champion Joe Louis. Once again Braddock did not expect the win but pulled it off by winning in the tenth round. That was Braddock's last fight; he would make no comeback.

Braddock went on to serve as a captain in the U.S. Army Transportation Service during WWII.

He invested the monies made as a champ very wisely by becoming part owner in several lucrative business ventures. The biggest endeavor Braddock encountered involved a young Joe Louis. He made an agreement with Louis that if he lost the title, Louis would have to give Braddock 10 percent of his earnings for the next ten years. Fruitfully, Joe Louis would remain champion for the next twelve years.

While he was in the money, he gave back every penny he had, from when he was down-and-out, and more to aid in the relief of the unfortunates.

Braddock's accomplishment and poise inspired all, especially the folks who felt down-and-out and hit hard by the depression.

Joe Louis

1. Louis made an impressive New York debut by stopping Carnera in sixth before sixty thousand, June 1935.
2. King Levinsky fell in first round, August 1935.
3. Heavily-guarded Louis arrives for weigh-in a few hours before major bout with Max Baer.
4. Baer lasted four rounds with Joe on September 24, 1935.
5. Booming right drops Paulino Uzcudun. Louis says this was the hardest punch he ever landed.
6. Much of the credit for what Joe accomplished goes to his trainer and teacher, Jack Blackburn.
7. Famous deadpan face moves in at sparring partner as Joe trains for title bout with Braddock.

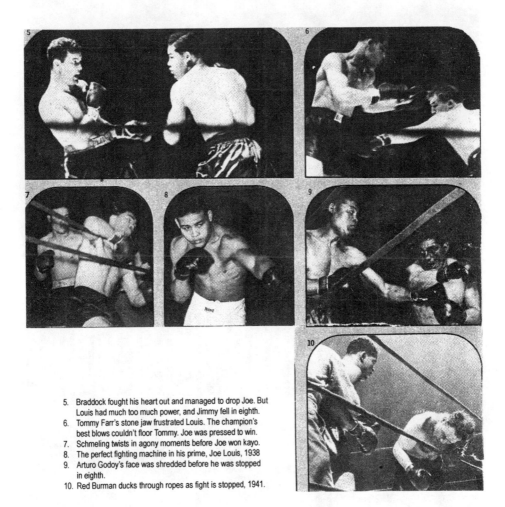

5. Braddock fought his heart out and managed to drop Joe. But Louis had much too much power, and Jimmy fell in eighth.
6. Tommy Farr's stone jaw frustrated Louis. The champion's best blows couldn't floor Tommy. Joe was pressed to win.
7. Schmeling twists in agony moments before Joe won kayo.
8. The perfect fighting machine in his prime, Joe Louis, 1938
9. Arturo Godoy's face was shredded before he was stopped in eighth.
10. Red Burman ducks through ropes as fight is stopped, 1941.

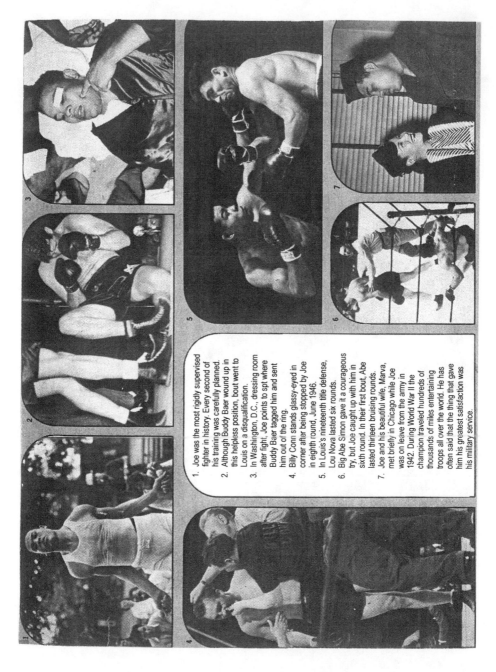

1. Joe was the most rigidly supervised fighter in history. Every second of his training was carefully planned.
2. Although Buddy Baer wound up in this helpless position, bout went to Louis on a disqualification.
3. In Washington, D.C., dressing room after fight, Joe points to spt where Buddy Baer tagged him and sent him out of the ring.
4. Billy Conn stands glassy-eyed in corner after being stopped by Joe in eighth round, June 1946.
5. In Louis's nineteenth title defense, Lou Nova lasted six rounds.
6. Big Abe Simon gave it a courageous try, but Joe caught up with him in sixth round. In their first bout, Abe lasted thirteen bruising rounds.
7. Joe and his beautiful wife, Marva, met briefly in Chicago while Joe was on leave from the army in 1942. During World War II the champion traveled hundreds of thousands of miles entertaining troops all over the world. He has often said that the thing that gave him his greatest satisfaction was his military service.

126

1. In September 1945, Sgt. Joe Louis and his old rival Pvt. Billy Conn get tremendous ovation in Madison Square Garden.
2. Out of the army, Louis and Conn weight in for return bout.
3. It has been five years since their historic first meeting, and Joe and Billy weren't near the fighters they used to be. They looked plump and tired. Louis chugged to an eighth-round TKO.
4. Tami Mauriello and Joe after Tami was kayoed in first round.
5. Most people thought Joe Walcott had earned decision over Louis in 1947. After he got the verdict, Louis, with an apologetic look, walked across ring to shake Walcott's hand.
6. Joe is met by benefactor Mike Jacobs at Miami airport, 1949.
7. Louis carries Ezzard Charles's gloves at Ezz's training camp.
8. Joe was deeply moved when his mother died in 1953 at sixty-nine.
9. Watching Joe try to wrestle in 1956 appalled his army of fans.

127

Joe Louis

Born: 1914-1981, Alabama
Weight: 198 lbs, 6'1"
Champion: 1937-1949

Won: 63   Lost: 3   Drew: 0   Knockouts: 49

A lot of boxing experts think that Joe Louis was the best heavyweight champion of all times. Whenever people talked about a fighting champion, the name Joe Louis comes up first. From the time he won the title in 1937, he was more than willing to give any contender a shot at this title. If they did a good job the first time, he was more than willing to give a rematch, which he always did better the second time around. When he retired in 1949, he had a record of twenty-five title defenses.

Joe was never what one would term a scientific boxer. He knew the mechanics of the ring, had a deadening punch and a devastating counterpunch. In all boxing heavyweight history, a choice few had enough power in both fists to knock a man unconscious. Joe was one of the few.

In his prime, Joe was a sleek six feet one, 195 to 200 pounds of coiled fury, shuffling slowly forward, patiently shooting out left jabs that struck with the impact of a battering ram, waiting for his opponent to make a mistake. That's about all you got from a young Louis—one mistake. After that one mistake, his fists would strike like a cobra, lefts and rights endlessly, ending only when an opponent was knocked out.

Born on May 14, 1914, on a Georgia cotton plantation, he was reared in the ghettos of Detroit. Growing up, Joe got into street-gang fights. His mother worried about him getting into trouble and had him take violin lessons.

Joe didn't care about the violin lessons and later started to miss his violin lessons that his mother was paying for. He was missing his lessons because he was accompanying a friend named Thurston McKinney to a local gymnasium.

Thurston McKinney was an amateur fighter, and he asked Joe to come to the gym and put the gloves on with him. Joe soon got serious and began training. Joe was in his teens and soon got involved in competition and tournaments. As an amateur he was great, winning fifty fights, losing four, with forty-one knockouts. He won the national AAU title in 1934.

Now twenty years old and with two years of amateur fighting, Joe was beginning to be noticed. Two businessmen from Detroit, John Roxborough and Julian Black, signed him to a professional contract. They then hired a fine lightweight of the early 1900s named Jack Blackburn to train him and keep him in line. It was a wise move. Joe had a soft spot for women and gambling, and Blackburn clamped down hard.

Much of the credit for Louis's success must go to Jack Blackburn. He polished his fighting style. He taught Joe leverage, balance, and proper stance. He taught and trained him with such fierce devotion that nobody dared interfere with Blackburn's methods.

With Roxborough, Black, and Blackburn, they led him cautiously into the professional ranks. His handler taught him to carry himself with dignity. The ban against black boxers, erected in Jack Johnson's day, still haunted black American boxers. After Jack Johnson, white promoters made no secret of their ban.

Louis's first professional fight was a kayo of Jack Kracken in one round on July 4, 1934. It was a main event for which he was paid fifty-two dollars. After this fight came better and better fighters but the same results, more and more knockouts. In his first pro year, he was 12-0.

The year 1935 was a good year for Joe. He won fourteen straight fights, mostly by early-round knockouts. Two of his knockouts were by former heavyweight champions.

On June 25, Joe was paid one hundred thousand dollars for knocking out former champion Primo Carnera in the sixth round. Then on September 24, Joe was paid $240,000 for knocking out former champion Max Baer in four rounds.

With beating these two former champions in 1935, all of boxing was aware of Joe Louis. He was knocking out opponents so often that he was called the Brown Bomber.

Joe won his first twenty-seven fights, twenty-four by knockouts. But champion Jim Braddock wasn't anxious to fight the seemingly unbeatable Louis, so Joe sought another former champion, Max Schmeling. Schmeling was a ten-to-one underdog. In this fight with Schmeling on June 19, 1936, Schmeling ripped right-hand counters over Louis's left jabs, knocked the shocked Louis out in the twelfth round. Early in the fight, Schmeling got in a sharp right over Louis's jab and put him down. This was Louis's first knockdown as a professional. Joe would say later that he never fully recovered from the blow that put him down in round four.

Before the Schmeling fight, Joe was sitting on top of the world. Everybody thought he was unbeatable with his boxing ability, punching power, and crowd appeal.

After losing to Schmeling, Joe became another heavyweight fighter. He now had to regain the prestige that he had lost with the Schmeling fight. To do this he had to win and win and win by the route of knockouts. That was what he was doing before the Schmeling fight.

Joe wanted a rematch with Schmeling immediately, but his managers wanted to go the route to the champion Jim Braddock and not Schmeling. They also wanted to make sure this time he was ready for Schmeling.

To get his name big in the boxing world again, he signed to fight yet another former champion Jack Sharkey on August 17, 1936. Joe easily won this fight in three rounds.

Joe would go on; and with eleven straight fights, mostly by knockout, he was on his way to fighting Jim Braddock for the championship on June 22, 1937.

With the championship fight against Braddock, it was one of the few times that the challenger was favorite to win over the champion.

Braddock put up a game fight, even knocking Louis down in the first round, but Louis landed too many solid left hooks and right hands to the jaw. He slowed Braddock down, puffed his eyes, and split his lip. In the eighth round, Joe landed a left to the body and a hard right to the chin. The referee counted him out. Joe said after the fight, "I want Schmeling. I ain't no champion till I beat Schmeling."

When Joe won the title, he became the second black champion since Jack Johnson. It lifted the hearts of black Americans. Many young black boys listened on radio, took heart that someday he could be a fighter and a hero to his people as Joe Louis was.

From the time Joe had his first professional fight, he never fought a single preliminary bout. All throughout his career were main-event fights.

For two years Joe waited for Schmeling, knocking out everybody else. Finally he got Schmeling in the ring on June 22, 1938. With Germany fighting in Europe, the whole world wanted this fight. Schmeling, being from Germany and a personal friend of Hitler's, represented everything that Americans disliked.

Louis had the whole country depending on him to beat Schmeling. Whites who didn't like blacks were for the black fighter. President of the United States, Franklin Roosevelt, met with him in the White House and said, "Joe, we're depending on those muscles for America." To Joe, it was personal because he wanted the rematch with the only fighter that beat him. He was the first black American to achieve the status of national hero.

The fight took place at Yankee Stadium where over seventy thousand people were present. It didn't last long. Louis's plan going into the fight was to go all out and get it over with fast.

Joe almost killed the startled Schmeling with vicious rights to the head, rib crushing blows to the body. Schmeling only had a chance to throw a couple of punches. Joe pounded him helplessly on the ropes. He went down four times. While down the fourth time, Schmeling's trainer threw in the towel, but the referee continued to count him out in round one. Joe said, "Now you can call me champ."

After Louis's first-round win over Schmeling, he won his next two fights in 1939 by first-round knockouts over John Henry Lewis and Jack Roper. With the first-round win over these two fighters and Schmeling, he became the only heavyweight champion to ever win three consecutive championship bouts by first-round knockout.

Since winning the title from Braddock in June 1937, for the next two years Louis had cleaned up all of the heavyweight contenders like no other champion had. He had beaten five former champions—Primo Carnera, Max Baer, Jack Sharkey, Jim

Braddock, and Max Schmeling. At this time in 1939, there was not a man on earth who could be a threat to his title.

Joe's first really tough fight had come on his seventh defense of his title against Two Ton Tony Galento on June 28, 1939. Galento was a short five feet and nine but heavy 225 pounds of out-of-shape body. He never trained right, drank a lot of beer, and ate everything; but he was a good fighter with a good hard left hook.

The very first round he landed a thunderous left hook to Louis's jaw. Louis was hurt, his legs buckled as he had to cover up. Galento chased Louis the rest of the round, winning the first round.

The second round was different as Joe landed hard rights and lefts with jolting punches. Galento went down in the round and was badly hurt in the round. The bell helped save him. At the end of the round, he was bleeding profusely from the right eye, nose, and mouth.

In the third round, Joe continued his vicious attack, when suddenly Galento landed another hard left hook. It landed on Louis's chin, knocking him down. Joe got up, not seriously hurt.

Starting the fourth round, Joe wanted to end the fight. Joe had Galento trapped on the ropes and hammered away at him. Galento was now helpless; and the referee, Arthur Donovan, had to stop it.

One of Joe's major problems that plagued his trainer throughout his career was the recruitment of sparring partners; Louis was a murderous puncher. The sparring partners would wear both a head-and-body protector.

In December 1939 Louis and promoter Mike Jacobs started a fight of the month, which got better fame as the Bum of the Month.

For six straight months, Joe had defeated all contenders rather easily by knockouts. By June, Mike Jacobs had problems finding a suitable opponent for Louis. For Joe's seventh fight in seven months, Jacobs came up with Billy Conn, a light-heavyweight champion. This would be Joe's toughest fight of the Bum of the Month campaign.

During the fight Conn fought a great fight using his speed and sharp left hooks. As the fight went on, it was Conn who was winning on points late in the fight. Louis was looking like a tired fighter.

In the twelfth round, Conn almost put Louis down with a left hook to the chin that caused Joe's legs to buckle.

Starting the thirteenth round, Joe was told he was losing the fight by Blackburn and needed a knockout. Conn, for his twelfth-round showing, was looking for the knockout instead of playing it safe for the final few rounds.

Conn tried to go toe-to-toe with Joe and lost to the more powerful champion. Joe threw a powerful right that hurt Conn and then followed up with rights and lefts to knock Conn out in the thirteenth round.

Joe joined the army in 1942. By this time he had destroyed twenty-one challengers since winning the title.

He was a solid American who loved his country and put it where his heart was. While in the service, his job was being in the field of morale entertainment; he gave boxing exhibitions and refereed bouts between other soldiers at various camps.

Joe had two championship fights in 1942. He knocked out Buddy Baer in one round and donated his purse to Naval Relief Fund. He then knocked out Abe Simon in six rounds and donated his purse to Army Relief Fund.

Joe came out of the army in 1946. He had lost valuable time in his career by being in the service. When he came out, he was now a puffy thirty-three-year-old and was never the same fighter again like he was before he went into the service. He would have four more fights before retiring from the ring as champion.

One of the four fights he had was the first fight with Jersey Joe Walcott, which he was lucky to win the decision. It was on December 5, 1947, when Walcott had floored Louis twice. So certain was Joe that he lost, he left the ring before the decision was announced and had to be called back to have his hand raised.

Louis and Walcott had a rematch in June 1948. This time Joe knocked Walcott out in the eleventh round. This would be Joe's last fight before retiring.

Joe denied no challenger an opportunity, and if they put up a good fight the first time, as Billy Conn and Joe Walcott did, he gladly give them a second chance. In no return match in his career did Joe fail to improve on his first showing. If the challenger went the distance and lost the decision the first time, he was knocked out convincingly the second fight.

Joe was one of the well liked of all the champions. He proved himself in the ring as a fighting champion who avoided no one. He not only won the acclaim of his own people, but he also changed the image of the black American in the eyes of millions around the world. Unlike the controversial first black champion Jack Johnson, Louis was a fine champion and citizen.

In 1949 Joe knew he didn't have it anymore. On March 1, 1949, he announced his retirement as the undefeated heavyweight champion of the world.

In his twelve years as champion, he was a feared knockout puncher. At the time he retired, he had twenty-five title defenses; no champion before him had half that many. Out of his twenty-five times defending his title, he only went the distance three times. Of the twenty-five fights, seven were by knockouts in the first round.

It would have been a great ending to his career, except that his career wasn't over. He came out of retirement in September 1950.

The number one reason for his comeback was taxes. He was way behind on his taxes even while being champion. Being retired in 1949, Joe had different companies, made exhibition tours, and made good money. The problem was the more money he made, the more the government took. Just paying the interest and penalties alone was fifty thousand dollars yearly.

In 1950 the government had filed a fifty-nine-thousand-dollar tax lien against Joe. They froze any money he could get from his properties. He couldn't sell any properties unless the government received the money.

With the money problem he was having, he signed to fight the champion Ezzard Charles, September 27, 1950. Joe was now thirty-six years old and only a shadow of the real Joe Louis. He though his punching power could beat Charles's boxing ability.

In the fight Charles wore Joe out and cut him up. Charles's jab was working; Joe's wasn't fast enough, and his reflexes were rusty, and his coordination was off. From the seventh round, he knew he didn't have it. Charles retained his title, winning on a fifteen-round decision.

Joe could be outboxed, and he could be hit. Until the twilight of his career, he was never up against a fighter with both qualities, though at times he was extended and even dropped to the canvas. He was floored by Jim Braddock, Max Schmeling, Buddy Baer, Tony Galento, and Jersey Joe Walcott, thus exhibiting one important weakness in his makeup.

After the Charles fight, Joe knew he was an old fighter but a dangerous fighter and that the other heavyweight contenders weren't as good as Charles. He also knew that no matter, he was a symbol to the American people, and the government still wanted their money. Joe still wanted the heavyweight title and the money it would bring.

So Joe continued to fight, winning eight bouts in a row. Then he was signed to fight Rock Marciano on October 26, 1951. At this time Marciano was the new great white hope.

At the time it was a fight Joe did not want; he wanted more a shot at the world title held by new champion Jersey Joe Walcott. But Joe also knew that Marciano was very popular, and it was a money-making fight. He couldn't turn down three hundred thousand dollars for one fight because he still owed the government one million dollars and about one hundred thousand dollars a year in interest.

In the fight it was pretty much even, up to the seventh round. Joe's jab was working good; Marciano was strong and fighting a brawl-like fight. In the eighth round, Joe's age caught up with him; his legs were gone. Marciano knocked Joe down twice in the eighth; the second one put him out, and the referee stopped the fight. This would be Joe Louis's last fight. He was now thirty-seven years old.

When it was over, Joe had a total of seventy-six fights; won seventy-three, fifty-nine by knockout; and lost only three times, twice during an abortive comeback that he began in 1950, a year after he retired.

During Louis's boxing career, he earned almost five million dollars in the ring. When he retired from the ring for the last time, he owed more than a million dollars in taxes to the United States government. Most of his money problems with money came from poor investments, high living, and by the people he trusted. People were into Joe, and the money was never accounted for.

After his days in the ring, Joe used the Joe Louis name to make money. Louis died in 1981 at the age of sixty-seven of a heart attack. He was buried at Arlington National Cemetery, a ground sacred to Americans who come here to honor their military dead.

Title Vacant: March 1, 1949-June 22, 1949

The third title vacant happened when Joe Louis retired as champion on March 1, 1949. The boxing promoter Jim Norris and the National Boxing Association (NBA) agreed that Jersey Joe Walcott and Ezzard Charles were the most likely contenders to fight for the title.

On June 22, 1949, Ezzard Charles defeated Jersey Joe Walcott by a fifteen-round decision to become the new heavyweight champion of the world.

Ezzard Charles

1. The sensational knockout of Archie Moore by Charles in eighth round in Cleveland, January 1948
2. When Sam Baroudi (left) died after kayo, Ezzard never fully recovered from the shock.
3. Charles and Joe Walcott examine gloves they wore in bout, which gave Ezzard NBA title.
4. Ezzard stopped Gus Lesnevich to retain title.
5. Charles won universal recognition as champion by beating a tired Joe Louis, 1950.
6. Heavyweight king Charles beat light-heavy king Joey Maxim in fifteen rounds in Chicago, 1951.
7. Ezzard was too good for Rex Layne in 1953.

Jersey Joe Walcott heads to the floor after fielding a left hook to the jaw in the ninth round of his second fight with Charles. Walcott beat the count but lost a unanimous fifteen-round decision.

Coley Wallace feels the power in Charles's right hand during their scheduled ten rounder in 1953. Charles stopped Wallace in the final round of the bout held in San Francisco.

A rare photo of Charles and legendary basketball player Wilt Chamberlain, taken while Chamberlain was still a student at Philadelphia's Overbrook High School.

Editor Nat Fleischer presents a beaming Charles with his *Ring Magazine* championship belt.

This is how Charles looked after fifteen give-and-take rounds with heavyweight champion Rocky Marciano. Although Charles failed in his bid to regain the title, his brave stand against the murderous-hitting Brockton Blockbuster earned him much admiration and a rematch.

140

Ezzard Charles

Born: 1921-1975, Georgia
Weight: 185 lbs., 6'
Champion: 1949-1951

Won: 93   Lost: 25   Drew: 1   Knockouts: 52

Ezaard Charles was a quiet man and a great heavyweight fighter. He got little credit for his ability because he became champion after the great Joe Louis had retired from the ring.

Charles was considered a top-notch boxer with speed, stamina, a stinging punch with some power to back it up, an excellent boxer and a counterpuncher, but no killer instinct. He was a very crafty fighter whose brain put him on top.

Growing up, Charles wanted to be a champion, and his idol was Joe Louis who was champion when he first started boxing. Fighting as an amateur, Charles was great. He started fighting as a welterweight. He had the best amateur record of any fighter in history as a foundation for his professional career. The experience proved to be a great advantage as he rolled up an astonishing list of 102 victories. Charles won ten different amateur titles, including the Golden Gloves champion in the middleweight division.

Charles was drafted into the army where he served three years. He continued to fight and had great success. He won every championship he competed in and every fight he fought in.

Turning pro in 1940, Charles was an outstanding middleweight and light heavyweight while working his way up to the heavyweight division. The light-heavyweight champion Gus Lesnevich would not give him a title fight.

By the late '40s, after not getting a title fight in the light-heavyweight division, his best weight was in the 180s. Charles began setting his mind on fighting Joe Louis for the heavyweight title.

Charles was on his way beginning in 1946, when he defeated Archie Moore by a decision. Then he defeated two top contenders: Lloyd Marshall by knockout and Jimmy Bivins by a decision. In rematches against Bivins and Archie Moore, Charles would win both by knockouts.

After the three great wins over Moore, Bivins, and Marshall, next came the fight with Sam Baroudi in 1948. Before the Baroudi fight, Charles was looked as a fighter with a deadly punch, and he fought with savagery.

In the fight with Sam Baroudi, Baroudi died from the fight. Charles took the death of Baroudi very hard. Charles never had the killer instinct again; he would have thoughts in the ring in other fights, he had struggled with himself, and he even said he would retire from the ring; he was a very upset fighter who was punishing himself.

A lot of different people, even Baroudi's family, talked to Charles and talked Charles into not retiring from the ring and to continue his boxing career. They knew it wasn't his fault and that he still had a great career to finish.

Charles changed his mind and continued to fight. As he continued to fight, and it would be hard for him to go after a person for the kill, when he knew that the other fighter was already hurt and that he could inflict more injury. He still had Baroudi's death on his mind. It was now that many boxing fans thought that Charles didn't have the killer instinct; the power was gone.

Charles got his big break when Joe Louis retired as champion in 1949. By now mainly because of Louis's commendable conduct, not only as a fighter but also as an American, black fighter had broken through with ex-precedent success.

An elimination tournament was held to fill the title vacancy left by Joe Louis's retirement. Ezzard Charles and Jersey Joe Walcott were the top contenders at the time, both black fighters. It was agreed that the new champion would be the winner of the Charles and Walcott fight. The fight took place at the Chicago Stadium on June 25, 1949. Charles won the fight on a fifteen-round decision and became the new heavyweight champion of the world.

Charles had a poor press while he was champion. This attitude was reflected in the public's reaction to Charles as a champion. They thought that he was dull but a good fighter.

After winning the title, Charles had three successful defenses of his title, all by knockouts. One was against Gus Lesnevich, the same light-heavyweight champion who would not give him a title fight, but he was still having trouble being accepted as champion.

From the time Charles won the title, everybody wanted Joe Louis to come out of retirement and get his title back from Charles. A lot of the boxing fans still thought that the unbeaten retired-champion Joe Louis was the real champion. The only way boxing fans would think of Charles as champion was for him to fight and beat the retired Joe Louis, who hadn't fought in two years but was still looked upon as the undefeated champion by many.

At this time in 1950, Joe Louis was having big problem with his taxes and needed money badly. Louis thought he could beat Charles and regain his title.

Charles wanted the fight to prove that he was not only the champion to some boxing fans but the undisputed champion of all.

The Charles and Louis fight took place on September 27, 1950. Louis was thirty-six years old, weighing 218 pounds; Charles was twenty-nine and weighing 183 pounds; even though Louis had been retired for two years, he was still a 2-1 favorite to win.

Louis was past his prime for this fight and was no match for Charles in the fight. Charles was much too fast and pounded Louis into a bleeding helpless fighter and won a one-sided decision. Charles felt bad about the fight, being it was Joe Louis, because of his love for Louis; Charles would say that "this was his most distasteful win of his career."

After beating Louis, Charles defended his title four more times. He knocked out Nick Barone and Lee Oma and then two unanimous decisions over Jersey Joe Walcott and Joey Maxim.

Charles's ninth defense of his title was against Jersey Joe Walcott. He had beaten Walcott on two previous occasions. This was their third fight. In this one Walcott knocked Charles out in the seventh round and became the new champion. Charles had successfully defended his title nine times. He had fought back gamely against the insinuation that he was not a real champion.

After losing his title to Walcott, Charles fought for the title three more times. He lost the rematch with Walcott by a decision. In 1954 he had two championship fights with Rocky Marciano, losing the first fight on a hard-fought fifteen-round decision. His showing was so good that the thirty-three-year-old Charles got a rematch in three months with Marciano. This time Marciano put Charles out in the eighth round.

He continued to fight until 1959. He holds the record for having forty-three bouts after losing the title. With 122 professional fights, he had more than any other world heavyweight champion.

After Charles lost his world heavyweight to Jersey Joe Walcott, he dropped a big load off his chest. He enjoyed being champion, but he was relieved from the strain one undergoes when he is a titleholder.

Charles said, "From the time that I whipped Jersey Joe Walcott to win the title until the moment I was counted out in my Pittsburgh battle, I had to face a rather hostile crowd. No matter how good I fought, no matter who my opponent was and how wide my margin of victory, I was never treated as I felt I should have been, and only because in the minds of the average fight fan I did not measure up to the standard of Joe Louis, Jack Dempsey, or Gene Tunney, but I never pretended to be up to that standard. However I was the world champion. I was the best heavyweight among all those who attempted to gain the crown that Louis had worn, and such, I simply couldn't understand the attitude of the fans who booed every time I fought."

Other heavyweight champions have had this same kind of hurt. Former champions like Jim Corbett and Gene Tunney were like Charles, filled with scorn and backslaps following a great champion. That's the way the history of boxing goes. No matter how great, it took years of headaches and heartaches before each received his fighting dues.

After Charles's boxing career was over, he turned to wrestling. As a wrestler he wasn't that successful, and he went to work for the City of Cincinnati.

Jersey Joe Walcott

1. Quick kayo of Tom Gomez in '46 made Joe a contender.
2. Walcott wasn't nearly as effective against Joe Louis in their second title bout as he had been in the first.
3. Harold Johnson crumbled in third round at Philadelphia, 1950. But many complained they didn't see Walcott land kayo blow.
4. Jersey Joe went to Germany in 1950 to batter big Hein Ten Hoff to defeat in ten rounds. It was a dull fight.
5. Walcott still can't believe he's champion as he is interviewed after kayoing Charles in Pittsburgh, 1951.
6. The thirty-eight-year-old champ again beat Charles in 1952.
7. For thirteen bloody rounds, Walcott strained to save his crown from Marciano. But he finally collapsed, September 1952.

Jersey Joe Walcott

Born: 1914-1994, New Jersey
Weight: 197 lbs., 6'
Champion: 1951-1952

Won: 50   Lost: 18   Drew: 1   Knockouts: 30

Jersey Joe was one of the best conditioned fighters of all time. At the time, he won the title at thirty-seven to be the oldest champion to hold the title; his muscles were just as hard as they were at twenty-one, and he still had the speed and drive of a younger fighter and the body of a younger fighter.

As a fighter Walcott was a clever boxer, good punch, good footwork, and always in good condition.

Walcott's real name was Arnold Cream, and he grew up in a large family of twelve. He had to quit school at age thirteen to go to work and bring some money in by working odd jobs after his father had died. Walcott started working out at the Battling Moc Gym, and he would turn pro at sixteen in 1930. He started out fighting as a lightweight. He won his first fight by a knockout in the first round.

Walcott won his first eleven fights, fighting under the name of Arnold Cream. His people and he felt he should change his name. They chose the name Joe Walcott after the great champion Joe Walcott who had fought years ago.

By the time he was thirty, he quit the ring because he wasn't doing great in the ring. He quit the ring to have a steady job. After losing to Abe Simon in 1940, he came back four months later and quit again. He remained retired for the next three years.

Walcott was receiving a $9.50 weekly relief checks from the Camden, New Jersey, board for a year and a half to feed his wife and six children. He had several comebacks; he quit the ring often because of the small pay he received.

He had to work on construction jobs, drive trucks, and mix cement. By being over thirty, he also thought he was too old, and he had lost some fights.

A change for Walcott came in 1944 when a manager named Felix Bocchiccio induced Walcott to get back into boxing and promised to care for his family until he could make enough to feel secure. Bocchicchio had a partner named Joe Webster of the Camden Athletic Club, and between them they got Walcott to accept the offer. This would be his big and final comeback that would lead to the title. The local promoter also wanted Walcott to come back. He promised him six well-paid fights. Walcott ran through those fights.

What happened after coming back into the ring in 1944 is ring history. He began to win very consistently. Having big wins over Lee Oma, Tom Gomez, and Joey Maxim, who later became the light-heavyweight champion, made him a top contender. Those wins helped him very quickly become a top contender to fight Joe Louis for the title. During this time his new manager was Felix Bocchicchio.

In 1947 Walcott got to fight Joe Louis for the heavyweight championship. Walcott fought a great fight. He knocked Louis down in the first round with a right to the chin and flooring Louis again the fourth round. At the end of the fifteenth round of fighting, everybody who saw the fight — the referee, and even Joe Louis — thought that Walcott had won the fight by a safe margin. What happened in the judging was that two judges gave the decision to Louis, so Louis won by a split decision.

Except for it being a championship lost to Joe Louis, it wasn't that bad. Because of his great showing, he was set as a top contender, which would pay off later when Louis retired. It also set him up for high-paying rematch with Louis. Even better from that day on, he never had to worry about the wolves hanging around his door. He now had a good home and a huge bank account.

The Louis and Walcott rematch happened on June 25, 1948. In the rematch with Louis three months later, Walcott knocked Louis down again in this fight in the early rounds and had Louis's eye swollen; but in round eleven, Louis caught Walcott in the corner and pounded him till he could not continue as the referee counted Walcott out; Walcott wasn't as affected as the first fight.

When Joe Louis retired as champion in 1949, Walcott fought Ezzard Charles for the vacant title; Walcott lost to Charles in this fight for the title. This was Walcott's third loss in a row for the title. Ezzard Charles gave Walcott a rematch and again beat Walcott by a decision.

In 1951 it was Charles and Walcott's third match. This was Walcott's fifth chance to win the championship; Walcott was fighting his age and knew this was it, and he had to get Charles early. Boxing experts thought he was too old to win the title and thought that Walcott should have been retired.

Walcott fought a cagey-type-attack fight and went after Charles full blast. He rocked Charles at the close of the third round with a couple of hard rights.

In the sixth round, Charles appeared to realize that time was running out, and he was losing on points. He stepped up his game and landed more punches with left hooks, moving good around the ring. Walcott was fighting a gain fight, being well trained and fighting sharp, as Charles was fighting an unimpressive fight.

In the seventh round, Walcott ripped Charles with a left hook; Charles went down. He took a count of nine, tried to get up, and tumbled over on his head. At thirty-seven, Walcott was the oldest champion to win the title. With his two losses to Joe Louis and the two earlier losses to Ezzard Charles for the championship, it took Walcott all thirty-seven years to win the title on his fifth try.

After winning the title, he gave Charles a return match and repeated it by beating Charles again in their fourth and last fight. When Walcott as champion, he was a champion with lots of experience, tricks, and jolting power.

In September of 1952, Walcott defended his title against Rocky Marciano. They fought thirteen bloody rounds. Walcott was leading on points and trying to save his title from the pressing Marciano. Marciano got in a short right on Walcott's chin and knocked him out, and a new champion was crowned. Marciano gave Walcott a return match and took Walcott out in round one.

After retiring from the ring, Jersey Joe devoted a lot of his time working with underprivileged youths and with New Jersey boxing.

Rocky Marciano

1. Rex Layne (rt) was Marciano's thirty-sixth consecutive victim, falling in sixth round, July 1951.
2. Not even Rocky enjoyed the slaughter of old Joe Louis in 1951. Joe lasted until eighth round.
3. Flanked by promoter Jim Norris, with champion Joe Walcott looking on, Marciano signs to fight Harry Matthews (left). Harry fell in two.
4. Lee Savold pulls away from Rocky's left hook.
5. and 6. Rocky's fist distorts Joe Walcott's face before Joe's defeat in thirteenth made Marciano champion. The happy winner, still undefeated.
7. Marciano and Luis Firpo ham it up in 1953.

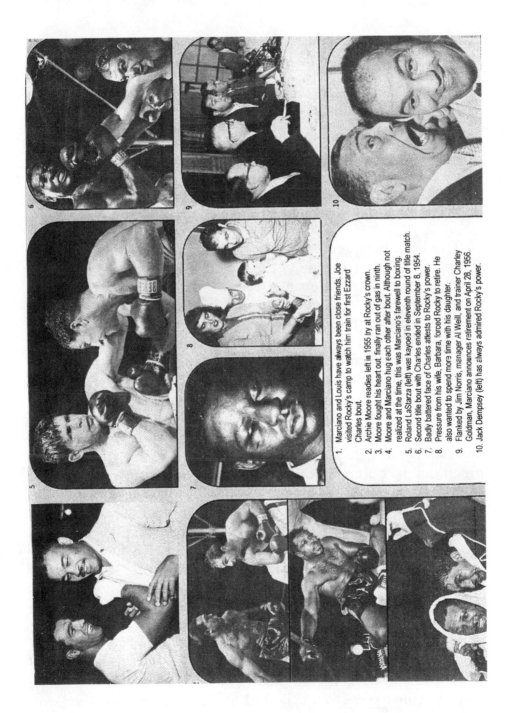

1. Marciano and Louis have always been close friends. Joe visited Rocky's camp to watch him train for first Ezzard Charles bout.
2. Archie Moore readies left in 1955 try at Rocky's crown.
3. Moore fought his heart out, finally ran out of gas in ninth.
4. Moore and Marciano hug each other after bout. Although not realized at the time, this was Marciano's farewell to boxing.
5. Roland LaStarza (left) was kayoed in eleventh round of title match.
6. Second title bout with Charles ended in September 8, 1954.
7. Badly battered face of Charles attests to Rocky's power.
8. Pressure from his wife, Barbara, forced Rocky to retire. He also wanted to spend more time with his daughter.
9. Flanked by Jim Norris, manager Al Weill, and trainer Charley Goldman, Marciano announces retirement on April 28, 1956.
10. Jack Dempsey (left) has always admired Rocky's power.

151

Rocky Marciano

Born: 1923; Brockton, Massachusetts
Died: 1969
Champion: 1952-1956

Won: 49   Lost: 0   Draw: 0   Knockouts: 43

Credited with forty-three knockouts in forty-nine unbeaten fights, Marciano was one of the hardest-hitting champions that the heavyweight division had ever seen. He was a fighter with great courage and a tremendous kick in his right hand. Marciano was probably the most conditioned fighter of all the heavyweight champions. He was always in shape and trained, even when there was no fight at hand. He would train as hard for a lesser fighter as he would for a top contender.

Born in 1923, Marciano's parents were Italian immigrants. His parents named him Rocco Marchegiano. Growing up, Marciano's first love for a sport was baseball. He wanted to be a major-league baseball player. He was a power hitter, and he loved baseball so much that he quit school to work and to play semipro baseball.

Marciano went into the army in 1943. It was in the army that he started boxing. He fought as a heavyweight although he was small. Getting out of the army in 1946, he worked odd jobs and continued to box for small money.

As an amateur boxer, Marciano had only one loss, won by a decision, to Coley Wallace. He won the Golden Gloves of his area in New England fighting as a heavyweight. He caught the eye of Charley Goldman, trainer, and Al Weil, who became his manager. Neither Weil nor Goldman was impressed with what they saw. Initially, they saw a short fighter with two left feet, short arms, and very little boxing skills. They realized that he had punching power and figured that Rocky was worth taking a chance on.

Charley Goldman saw that Marciano had a natural punching ability. He transformed him from a crude willing youngster, with two left feet, into a deadly, effective fighting machine. He knew that Marciano was not a boxer. He got Marciano to move forward out of a crouch and trained him to throw shots to the belly, ribs, and forearms. Marciano was a ferocious puncher with a deadly right hand. At times he looked bad because he was so eager. He seemed unstoppable and could take a punch. At times he took four punches to land one of his. Marciano could be hit, hurt, cut, and even floored but could not be beaten.

Marciano was already twenty-four years old when he turned pro in 1947. This is late when it comes to boxing. Al Weil, his manager, had his name changed to Rocky Marciano to be easier to pronounce. He had his first fight on March 17, 1947. This fight against Lee Epperson ended with a third-round knockout. He won his first sixteen fights by knockouts. He wasn't fighting top fighters, but everyone knew that he had punching power in his right and that he knew how to take advantage of his left.

By 1950, Marciano was undefeated with a record of 25-0, with twenty-three knockouts. His twenty-sixth fight would be his toughest challenger up until then. This fight was against Roland LaStarza on March 24,1950. LaStarza was undefeated, with a record of 37-0 at the time, and favored to win. It was a tough fight with LaStarza winning the early rounds. Marciano had a fourth-round knockdown of LaStarza, and he scored hard punches in other rounds. Marciano won on a split decision. This win was a big jump for Marciano's drive for a title fight. Now that he was a contender, he would be getting bigger pay for his fights.

1951 was a good year for Marciano. He beat two top contenders. First he fought Rex Lane on July 12, 1951, who had beaten the present champion Jersey Joe Walcott. It would be Marciano's thirty-sixth undefeated fight. It would also be his biggest paying fight. In the fight, Marciano landed a lot of power punches to the head and body. He scored a sixth-round knockout of Lane. Marciano moved from contender to a top contender with this win.

Joe Louis was the second contender that Marciano fought that year. This fight was on October 26, 1951. Louis was on the comeback trail, having won eight straight fights, and was favored to win. This would be Marciano's thirty-eighth fight and the biggest one leading to the title.

Marciano trained very hard for his fight with the former great Joe Louis. Marciano had a small lead in points after seven rounds. He knocked Louis down with a left hook in the eighth round. Louis got up then went down a second time from a hard right, which ended the fight. The win over Lane and Louis and still being unbeaten in thirty-eights fights allowed Marciano to take a crack at the title. He was now the fighter to beat.

Jersey Joe Walcott, the present champion, agreed to fight Marciano for the title on September 23, 1952. Marciano was favored to win over the older champion Walcott because of his superior power and youth. Marciano needed all of the hard training that he did in this fight. Walcott dropped him in an early round with a hard left hook and piled up a big lead on points. This was a fight in which both fighters landed hard punches. Walcott was boxing better, and Marciano knew that only a knockout would earn him a victory. Marciano was just as tough and as dangerous as in the beginning. Marciano was taking the worst beating that he ever had, but he kept coming after Walcott. Both fighters were bleeding from cuts.

He began to narrow the gap in points with a relentless two-fisted attack. Knowing that he needed a knockout to win, Marciano came after Walcott in the thirteenth round. Out of the blue, Marciano knocked Walcott out with a blistering, powerful short right to the chin. Marciano was now the new world heavyweight champion after forty-three fight. He became the first white man to hold the title since 1937, a fifteen year gap.

Marciano would always give a return match if the first fight was a good one. The return fight with Walcott was on May 15, 1953, and everyone thought that they were going to see another great fight like the first fight that they had. It was not to be as Marciano came after Walcott with full speed, throwing every punch that he had. Walcott could not stop the punches, and as in the first fight, Marciano caught Walcott with a solid right in the first round, and the fight was over.

Marciano's second defense of his title was against Roland LaStarza on September 24, 1953. This was a fight that everybody wanted to see after Marciano had won the first fight in 1950 on a split decision. The fight was a tough fight. LaStarza led on points early in the fight, but Marciano started throwing hard punches and wearing LaStarza down. In the eleventh round, Marciano threw a lot of hard punches. A hard right knocked LaStarza out of the ring, but LaStarza beat the count. Marciano continued to pound away until the referee stopped the fight in the same eleventh round.

Marciano's third defense of his title was against Ezzard Charles on June 17, 1954. Charles was very sharp in the early rounds and even opened a cut on Marciano's left eye. Marciano started winning the later rounds and opened a cut on Charles's right eye. Marciano needed every punch to win over Charles, who was still strong and landing punches in the late rounds. Marciano won by a unanimous decision in the fifteenth round. This fight would be the only fight that Marciano would fight for fifteen rounds.

Everybody wanted to see the rematch of the Marciano-Charles fight. Marciano had said that the Ezzard-Charles fight was the toughest fight that he had ever been in. The rematch was set for September 17, 1954. The fight was all Marciano at first. Marciano was winning all of the rounds. He knocked Charles down in the second round, but Charles beat the count. Losing the first five rounds, Charles was just trying to fight off Marciano. In the sixth round, he split Marciano's nose real bad. It was so bad that Marciano and his corner knew that he could lose the fight over it. Not wanting the doctor or the referee to stop the fight because of his badly cut nose, Marciano came out, bleeding all over himself, for a quick knockout. He was also bleeding from a cut eye. Marciano knocked Charles down with a right. Charles got up but was dazed. Marciano stayed on him and knocked him down again for the knockout in the eighth round.

Marciano's last fight was against the current light-heavyweight champion Archie Moore on September 21.1956. This would be his sixth defense of his title. Moore fought a good fight and floored Marciano in the second round with a solid right. Marciano knocked Moore down two times in the sixth and eighth rounds as they continued to battle. In the ninth round, Marciano battered Moore in his corner and knocked him out.

After the Moore fight, Marciano looked over his array of challengers and realized that none were considered in his league. He had simply run out of worthy opponents. Pressured by his wife Barbara and wanting to spend more time with his daughter, Marciano decided to retire from boxing. He had made enough money to live comfortably, so at the age of thirty-three on April 27, 1956, Marciano officially retires. This is seven months after the Moore fight.

Marciano knew that Moore had floored him in his last fight and that Charles had damaged his features badly. Age was also becoming a factor, and training for a fight was harder for him. He was still strong, robust, and in exceptional condition. He could have remained champion for years.

Marciano was always the aggressor and came at you throwing punches at any part of your body. He would throw punches at the head, body, and arms doing damage. In some of his fights, he had actually broken bones and blood vessels in the opponents' arms, leaving them unable to lift their arms in defense.

Marciano was also short and squirt with the shortest reach of any heavyweight champion in history. He simply plowed straight ahead, swinging at anything that moved to do any damage. He was known for never giving his opponents breathing room, exacting relentless pressure until he wore them down and then clobbering them into submission.

Always in remarkable condition, he took great care of himself. He did not have a single bad habit, was ambitious and eager while fearing no man. Marciano could be hit, hurt, cut, and even floored; but he couldn't be beaten. The greatness about Marciano is that he was the only heavyweight champion to go unbeaten and untied at 49-0.

In 1969 Marciano ran, trained, and got back into the ring for a final time. This was a computerized fight with Muhammad Ali. This was not a real fight. They would box each other with Ali doing what he would usually do and Marciano doing what he would usually do in a fight. They punch each other but nothing serious. The computer would take all angles, blows, blocks, movements, and everything else and then determine from the data who would win the fight. In the end, Marciano won on a thirteen-round knockout of Ali. Marciano died about a month after the showing of the fight in an airplane crash.

Intelligent enough to have invested in various business opportunities, he was set for life. Years after his retirement, he began to become appreciated by the boxing community. He was one of the greatest heavyweight champions that ever lived.

Title Vacant: April 27, 1956-November 30, 1956

The third title vacant happened in 1956 when Rocky Marciano retired as the undefeated world champion. An elimination tournament was set up with the top contenders to fight for the vacant title.

Archie Moore received a bye in the tournament. Floyd Patterson and Tommy "Hurricane" Jackson fought, with Patterson winning. The win by Patterson set up for him to fight Archie Moore to find a new champion. Floyd Patterson won the fight with Moore to become the new heavyweight champion of the world.

Floyd Patterson

Floyd and his younger brother Ray review the film of Patterson's first fight with Ingemar Johansson, looking for chinks in the Swede's defense. Floyd was so shy he sometimes told people he was Ray to avoid attention.

Patterson and his manager-mentor Cus D'Amato talk things over at training camp. Although they split up later, by the time Patterson was thirty years old, D'Amato had helped him earn ten million dollars in purse money. D'Amato tried to prevent Patterson from fighting Sonny Liston.

1. After stopping Archie Moore in fourth, Patterson is declared champion in Chicago, November 30, 1956.
2. Roy Harris (left) lasted twelve rounds in unsuccessful attempt to lift Floyd's crown, 1958.
3. Pete Rademacher made history in 1957 when he fought for the title in his first pro bout. He was kayoed in sixth.
4. Floyd regains title from Ingemar Johansson.
5. Brian London is stopped in eleventh, 1959.
6. The famous peek-a-boo style of the champion
7. Patterson beats tough George Chuvalo, 1965.
8. A lonely man does roadwork on a lonely road.

Floyd Patterson

Born: 1935-2006
Weight: 195 lbs., 5'11"
Champion: 1956-1959, 1960-1962

Won: 55   Lost: 8   Drew: 1   Knockouts: 40

Floyd Patterson was a champion that was remembered for two things he had accomplished in the ring. When he won the title, he became the youngest heavyweight to win the title at twenty-one. The second thing that shocked the boxing world was Patterson being able to win his title back after losing it — not even the great Jack Dempsey or Joe Louis was able to do this.

In the ring, Patterson was a good fighter that consisted of very fast hands, excellent combination puncher, and great courage. The problem Patterson did have was that he got knocked down a lot.

Growing up, Patterson often got in trouble, which later caused him to go to reform school. After getting out of reform school, he started showing up at Cus D'Amato's gymnasium. Cus liked what he saw in Patterson in the gym. Cus started teaching Patterson at an early teen age how to protect himself in the ring and how to attack his opponent.

As the years went by, he taught Patterson more about boxing. Cus taught Patterson the peculiar peek-a-boo style of boxing that confused his opponents. This would be his trademark of fighting that helped him very quickly to climb the ladder to being a top contender to the title. The peek-a-boo style of boxing consisted of holding both hands in front of your face for protection and attack from there. As Patterson got better, Cus knew he had something special in a young Patterson.

As a amateur, Patterson won the Golden Gloves as a middleweight and as a light heavyweight in 1951 and 1952. He won the gold medal in the 1952 Olympics as a middleweight.

Turning pro in 1952, Floyd won thirty-five of his first thirty-six fights, losing only to Joey Maxim by an unpopular decision.

After Rocky Marciano retired in 1956 as the undefeated heavyweight champion of the world, it was Floyd Patterson and Archie Moore who fought each other in a tournament to find a new champion on November 10, 1956.

In the match against Moore, Moore was favored to win because of his fine showing against Marciano and his experience. Patterson was leading Moore on points going into the fifth round. In the fifth, Patterson landed a powerful left hook to the jaw that sent Moore down. Moore got up and was again struck by another powerful left, sending him to the canvas for the last time as referee Frank Sikova counted Moore out, and Patterson became the new champion. In winning the title, he became the youngest fighter to win the heavyweight title, being twenty-one.

After winning the title, Patterson's first defense of the title was a rematch with Tommy "Hurricane" Jackson. In their first match, Patterson had won a split decision over Jackson. The rematch was all Patterson as he knocked Jackson down in the first round, in the second, and again in the ninth round. Referee Ruby Goldstein stopped the fight in the tenth round after Patterson had landed a smashing left and right to Jackson's jaw.

Patterson then signed to fight Peter Rademacher. Rademacher became the first amateur to challenge for the world title in his first fight. He had just won the gold medal in the heavyweight division in the 1956 Olympics. A lot of the boxing commission was against this fight, but it went on anyway.

On August 22, 1957, Peter Rademacher surprised a lot of the boxing fans by winning the first round and knocking Patterson down in the second round. Then it was all Patterson as he put Rademacher down in the third round, four times in the fifth, and finally putting Rademacher away in the sixth round.

After the Rademacher fight, Patterson would later get a thirteen-round TKO over Roy Harris and an eleventh-round knockout over Brian London. For the three years he would be champion, he had four successful title defenses.

During Patterson's era as champion, this was the age when money was made, not from the live audience, but from TV.

Patterson's fifth defense of his title was against Ingemar Johansson on June 26, 1959. In the fight Johansson knocked Patterson down seven times in winning the fight by a TKO in three rounds to become the new heavyweight champion.

Before the fight with Johansson, boxing fans thought Patterson was a good fighter. After he lost to Johansson and being floored seven times, boxing people was now saying that Patterson had a glass jaw and was an overweight light heavyweight and other negative things.

Not having his title now, Patterson set out to prove everyone wrong and got a rematch to win his title back. He not only wanted his title back, but he also wanted revenge for the humiliation he had suffered in losing his title.

One year later on June 20, 1960, it was Johansson and Patterson again. Not many boxing experts thought Patterson could win his title back. They knew that other greater champions before him had lost their title and tried to get it back but failed to rewin their title.

Throughout the fight, Patterson landed jabs, hooks, and hard rights. In the fifth round, Patterson landed a long left to Johansson's chin, putting him down for the count of nine. After getting up, Patterson pounded the body and then landed a jolting left hook on the chin, sending Johansson down-and-out for the count, to become the first champion in heavyweight division to regain his title.

Patterson's second reign as champion lasted for two years. He had a third fight with Johansson that he won by a sixth-round knockout and a fourth-round knockout over Tom McNeeley.

During the time Patterson was winning the last two fights with Ingemar Johansson and the other fights he had, Sonny Liston, manager, said that Cus was protecting Patterson from fighting Liston. Liston was the number one contender to the title, and he was knocking out everyone he fought. Cus did not want Patterson to defend his title to the hard-hitting Sonny Liston.

So Liston had to wait. Boxing during this era, you did not lose your title when you did not fight the number one contender. Patterson wanted the fight because the boxing fans were calling for it and because they said he had no chance of beating Liston.

Finally on his third defense, Patterson fought Sonny Liston on August 25, 1962. Liston won the title by knocking Patterson out in the first round; Liston and Patterson fought a rematch. The rematch was no different as Liston once again won by a first-round knockout.

After being defeated by Liston the second time, he kept fighting, winning five straight fights. In the five fights, Patterson defeated two top-rank fighters Eddie Machen and George Chuvalo. This earned him a championship fight with Muhammad Ali in 1965. The fight was no fight as Ali easily won in twelve rounds.

After losing his title fight to Ali, Patterson was planning on retiring from the ring. He changed his mind and fought the English champion Henry Cooper, whom he knocked out in fourth round. Still a contender in 1968, Patterson was involved in the elimination tournament to find the successor to the title that was taken from Muhammad Ali. In the tournament, Patterson lost a close decision to Jerry Quarry.

Before retiring in 1972, Patterson would fight another fight with Ali in 1972. In the rematch with Ali, Patterson got knocked out in the eighth round.

As champion Patterson showed class both inside and outside the ring. A very sensitive man, he sometimes was more concerned for the safety of his opponents than for himself. After Patterson retired, he worked as the commissioner for the New York Athletic Commission.

Ingemar Johansson

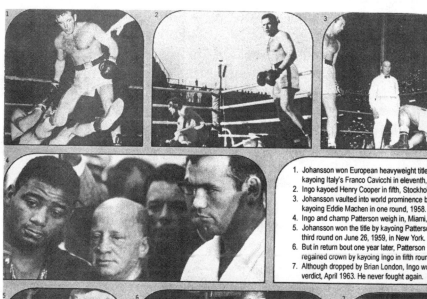

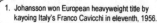

1. Johansson won European heavyweight title by kayoing Italy's Franco Cavicchi in eleventh, 1956.
2. Ingo kayoed Henry Cooper in fifth, Stockholm.
3. Johansson vaulted into world prominence by kayoing Eddie Machen in one round, 1958.
4. Ingo and champ Patterson weigh in, Miami, 1961.
5. Johansson won the title by kayoing Patterson in third round on June 26, 1959, in New York.
6. But in return bout one year later, Patterson regained crown by kayoing Ingo in fifth round.
7. Although dropped by Brian London, Ingo won verdict, April 1963. He never fought again.

Ingemar "Ingo" Johansson

Born: 1932-2009, Sweden
Weight: 206 lbs., 6'
Champion: 1959-1960

Won: 26   Lost: 2   Drew: 0   Knockouts: 17

In 1959, Ingemar Johansson defeated Floyd Patterson to become the first Swede to hold the heavyweight title and the first European to hold the world heavyweight title since Primo Carnera of Italy twenty-five years previously.

Starting out he invented his own style. In the papers he was called Ingo. He liked to throw a short left hook to bring his opponent's guard down then throw a hard overhand right that would knock his opponent out.

Johansson was an average champion who held the championship for less than a year. He was an average boxer with a powerful right hand that led him to the title. He won most of his fights by knockouts by a shattering right that was called "Thor's Hammer."

At the age of sixteen, Johansson started his amateur career in 1948. He won the International Golden Gloves in 1951. He then went to the 1952 Olympics, making the finals as a heavyweight, where he was disqualified for not trying in his fight with Ed Sanders of the United States, ending up winning the silver medal. In eighty-nine amateur fights, Johansson won eighty fights with nine losses.

After the Olympics, Johansson was looked at as a coward and a disgrace by his Swedish people. The press charged him with not fighting in the second round and getting disqualified for it.

Johansson also turn pro after the Olympic in 1952. He won his first fight by a knockout. He fought mostly overseas and had great success. He would win twenty consecutive fights, thirteen by knockouts. As he started to climb the professional ladder, he captured the European heavyweight title on September of 1956 by knocking out Franco Cavicchi in thirteen rounds, winning all fights mostly by knockouts; he was soon being recognized all over the world and being offered big contract to fight.

As European heavyweight champion, he defended it successfully twice, with a fifth-round win over Henry Cooper and a thirteenth-round win over Joe Erskine.

The world found out who Johansson was on September 14, 1958, when he fought Eddie Machen. Machen at the time was one of the top contenders to the world title held by Floyd Patterson. Machen was also a 3-1 favorite to win.

Machen came to Sweden to fight Johansson. In the very first round, Johansson landed his famous Thor's Hammer right hand, and Machen was down and done with in the first round. This win over Machen made him the number one contender and got him the title fight with champion Floyd Patterson.

Johansson had unusual training methods. His training at the time would consist of swimming, dancing, and eating late-night snacks while training.

Patterson and Johansson sign to fight on June 26, 1959. Going into the fight with Patterson, most people had only heard of Johansson's powerful right hand but gave him almost no chance against Patterson. Up to the title fight, Johansson was undefeated in all his twenty-one fights; Patterson was a 4-1 favorite to win.

The first two rounds there wasn't a lot of action. In the third round from the start to end, it was clear this would be Johansson's fight. He landed a powerful right, his Hammer of Thor, that sent Patterson down. Patterson went down seven times in the round. It seems that every time Johansson's right landed, Patterson went down or was going to. Referee Ruby Goldstein stopped the bout in 2:03 of the third round, and Johansson became the new world champion.

By knocking Patterson down seven times in a round, Johnasson tied a record with Jack Dempsey, who had knocked Luis Firpo down seven times in 1923.

After beating Patterson for the world title, he gave up his European title. With the world title, he became a hero in Sweden.

He earn Associated Press Athlete of the Year Award, with Joe Louis being the only other fighter to win the award in 1935.

Johansson was a man of many trades; he made a fortune outside the ring, being a singer, actor, and a businessman.

The rematch with Patterson took place one year later in 1960. This time Johansson did not fight his best and lost by a knockout in the fifth round, losing his title.

Patterson and Johansson fought yet a third fight three months later. This time in their third fight, Johansson fought better and knocked Patterson to the floor twice in a great fight, but Patterson won in six rounds. This would be his last try at the world championship.

After his second loss to Patterson, he wasn't through fighting. Johansson went back home to fight. He had four more fights, winning all of them, and regained the European heavyweight title by beating Dick Richardson in eight rounds. In his last fight as a professional, he won a decision over Brian London in 1963 and retired as European champion at the age of thirty-one.

Johansson retired from the ring to go into business where he was very successful. Out of twenty-eight fights, he only lost the two fights to Floyd Patterson. *Ring Magazine* named Johansson one of the one hundred hardest punchers in history, and he was elected to the Boxing Hall of Fame. After his career was over, he still remained a hero in his country Sweden.

Charles "Sony" Liston

1. Mike DeJohn crumbles under impact of Liston's barrage in sixth. Bout took place in Miami, 1959.
2. Nino Valdez, kayoed in third, was Liston's eighteenth straight victim (sixteenth by kayo), Chicago, J959.
3. Sonny referees bout between Cleveland Williams (rt) and Dave Bailey in Houston, 1962.
4. London will never forget Sonny, who rode a horse through city streets during 1963 visit.
6. Sonny's favorite training exercise
7. Liston is deeply devoted to wife, Geraldine.
8. Left hook finds Patterson's face in first round.

Charles "Sonny" Liston

Born: 1932-970, Arkansas
Weight: 220 lbs., 6'1"
Champion: 1962-1964

Won: 50   Lost: 4   Drew: 0   Knockouts: 39

Sonny Liston was known as one of the most ferocious, feared heavyweight champion of all time. He was identified as a powerful and menacing heavyweight champion.

Liston weighed 220 lbs., with a seventeen-and-a-half-inch neck and had fists measuring fifteen inches in size. He was a bulky boxer that was fast on his feet. He delivered ferocious punches and destructive jabs. He had an eighty-four-inch reach, which was considered to be one of the longest of any heavyweight champion. His left hook was a lethal weapon with an uppercut that could lift you off your feet. He was treacherous when attacking his opponent's body, but he could withstand a solid punch to the chin.

Sonny lived a hard tragic life, one filled with turbulent and despair. He was born in a Negro shantytown in poverty on an Arkansas farm, where his father was a field hand. At the age of thirteen, he ran away from home, only to run wild and live in the hated, segregated Jim Crow streets of St. Louis. He joined a bad crowd and in his own words was "just always looking for trouble." His attitude contributed to Sonny spending a lot of time in reform school.

In the aftermath of World War II, Liston was arrested over twenty times for various violent crimes, which include mugging and armed robbery. By 1950 Liston was simply number 63723, just another animated mug shot at the Missouri State Penitentiary at Jeffersonville. This prison was a brutal, vicious, dehumanizing old fortress that could serve as a monument to the inhumanity of man.

Sonny viewed the world as a cruel and forbidden place, except for when he was in the ring. So prison wasn't considered a bad experience. When Sonny turned eighteen, the Missouri penitentiary athletic director, Father Alous Stevens, encouraged Liston to take up boxing.

After serving his time, boxing became his life. As an amateur, he won the Golden Gloves championship in 1953, the same year that he turned pro. During his first thirty-five fights, he only lost one to Marty Marshall by a decision. Twenty-three were won by knockouts, seven (7) of these wins were fought against the top ten heavyweight contenders that lasted a total of fourteen (14) rounds.

These thirty-five fights were spread over a period of nine years. During that time also, two years were lost due to an assault on a police officer, which landed him back in prison to serve a nine-month sentence. Upon his release, he quit the ring for a year.

Liston waited two years as the number one contender before he was able to get a chance at a title fight with Floyd Patterson, the champion. His chance arrived on September 25, 1962. Like Joe Louis, Liston was one of the few challengers to enter a title fight with the betting odds in his favor.

Liston scored the third fastest heavyweight championship fight on record, two minutes and six seconds, in the first round. History was in the making. Liston started pounding Patterson from the start, taking control with jarring jabs and putting him in comparison with Joe Louis.

Patterson fought in a crouch, weaving with a display of caution with Liston pounding with both of those fifteen-inch hands into every part of Patterson's body, delivering accurate jabs. Patterson grabbed the ropes to support himself; with one arm supporting him against the ropes, he became a sitting target against the accurate jarring jabs of Liston.

Liston landed a hard left behind Patterson's ear, stunning him and making him immobile. Followed with a ferocious right to the body and left hook to the head, Patterson fell and couldn't get up. Liston became the new heavyweight champion of the world.

Liston once again proved that he was too powerful for Patterson in their rematch. He knocks Patterson down three (3) times winning the match in two minutes and ten seconds of the first round.

Even as champion, Liston had a few run-ins with the law, including drink-driving and impersonating an officer. The media coverage was hypocritical making Liston a target of more publicity than any other heavyweight champion at that time. Media coverage resulted in making Liston the most unpopular champion of all times. Despite Liston's courageous rise to the championship, he was not portrayed as possessing the qualities that make heroes like Dempsey or Joe Louis.

It hurt Liston terribly not to be accepted, hiding his pain behind a mean facade. It was his jailhouse mentally, his emotional survival, his armor against the world. Liston loved to stare people down and to intimidate lesser men by hurting people the way that he had been hurt.

February 1964, Liston defended his title against Cassius Clay, later know as Muhammad Ali. Liston's menacing appearance and past record both in and out of the ring made him seem invincible to beat and favorite 8-1 to win. Being such a large heavyweight who delivered strong hard hits, which resulted in his fights begin short anyway, Liston wanted a quick knockout in the fight with Clay.

From the start Liston came out throwing haymakers. Clay was constantly moving and dancing away from his punches causing Liston to miss and grow tired. Liston was not accustomed to throwing bummer punches without them landing on their mark. The third round Clay opened a cut under Liston's eye; this is the first time Liston has ever been cut in the ring.

Things became worse for Liston in the fourth round; he pulled a muscle in his shoulder while throwing a punch. Clay start throwing harder punches and continued to use his sharp jab that had been working all night causing Liston to tire even more.

At the start of the seventh round, Liston did not get off his stool complaining that he had damaged his shoulder and couldn't fight any longer. Liston stated later that he had sprung his shoulder. Many boxing fans still believed that Liston threw the fight. Before losing his title to Clay, Liston was considered unbeatable; some experts went as far as to rate him over Joe Louis as an all-around fighter. An 8-1 favorite over Clay, he was considered indestructible, yet he was unable to leave the stool for the seventh round.

After the first fight between Liston and Clay, no city wanted the rematch. It was finally held in a little town of Lewiston, Maine, on May 25, 1965. Liston was worn out in the first round from a "phantom" punch few people saw. Later a bill was introduced in Congress to ban the sport.

Liston would say about the second fight with Ali that he was knocked down with a sharp punch but was not hurt. He say as he lay on the canvas he looked up and saw Ali standing over him; he did not get up, feeling Ali was waiting to hit him with a great shot. Liston said he could see that the referee Jersey Joe Walcott could not control Ali, and he didn't get up for over seventeen seconds. By then the fight was over.

Liston destroyed himself after the second fight with Clay, who by now had changed his name to Muhammad Ali. Liston's marketability as a fighter had been destroyed; he was no longer ranked and never considered again as a major contender.

Liston made a comeback in winning fourteen fights, resulting in him receiving his ranking back, but by then he was through. The closest Liston ever came to another big money-making fight happened in Las Vegas on December 6, 1969, against Leotis Martin where Liston was knocked out in the ninth round. Liston's last fight occurred on June 29, 1970, in a ten-rounder-win TKO against Chuck Wepner.

On December 30, 1970, at the age of thirty-eight, Liston's body was found in his Las Vegas home from an apparent drug overdose. Investigator found drugs on the premises. It was said he may have been dead for about a week. At the time of his death, he was ranked the number 8 heavyweight by *Ring Magazine*.

Liston was in controversy from start to finish, losing two titled fights to Ali under suspicious circumstances and said to have mob connections. Liston's true abilities always remained questionable; even in death there was still controversy because of his two losses against Ali. Liston isn't given the credit he deserves.

Muhammad Ali

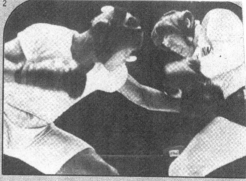

1. At the age of twelve, Cassius was already envisioning himself as a famous champion. Picture was taken in Louisville in 1954.
2. Clay, still a comparative unknown, talked himself into sparring with Ingemar Johansson at Miami in 1961 as Ingo trained for title fight with Patterson. Cassius more than held his own.
3. Sonny Banks (right) dropped Clay but suffered fourth-round TKO in New York, February 1962.
4. Cassius made world headlines when he stopped Archie Moore in fourth in Los Angeles, November 1962.
5. Moore's left eye was closed by Clay's jabs.

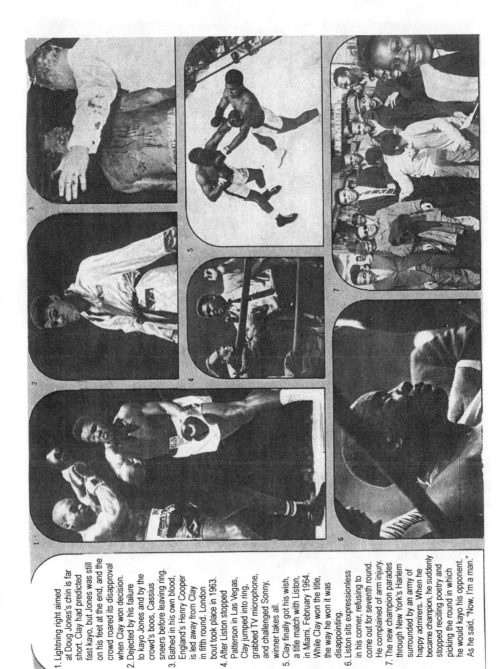

1. Lightning right aimed at Doug Jones's chin is far short. Clay had predicted fast kayo, but Jones was still on his feet at the end, and the crowd roared its disapproval when Clay won decision.

2. Dejected by his failure to kayo Jones and by the crowd's boos, Cassius sneers before leaving ring.

3. Bathed in his own blood, England's Henry Cooper is led away from Clay in fifth round. London bout took place in 1963.

4. After Liston stopped Patterson in Las Vegas, Clay jumped into ring, grabbed TV microphone, and challenged Sonny, winner takes all.

5. Clay finally got his wish, a title match with Liston, in Miami, February 1964. While Clay won the title, the way he won it was disappointing.

6. Liston sits expressionless in his corner, refusing to come out for seventh round. He complained of arm injury.

7. The new champion parades through New York's Harlem surrounded by an army of happy admirers. When he became champion, he suddenly stopped reciting poetry and picking the round in which he would kayo his opponent. As he said, "Now, I'm a man."

177

1. While Clay appears carefree and coldly confident, he's deadly serious about his training. He learned long ago that the fatal mistake most boxers make is to become lax about their condition.
2. Clay snarls angrily at Liston, who fell in first round at Lewiston, Maine, May 1965.
3. Drumming up publicity for future bout, Clay calls Patterson "rabbit" at Floyd's camp, January 1965.
4. George Chuvalo was Clay's victim in Toronto title bout, 1966.

Muhammad Ali (Cassius Clay)

Born: 1942, Kentucky
Weight: 210 lbs., 6'3"
Champion: 1964-1967, 1974-1978, 1978-1978

Won: 56   Lost: 5   Drew: 0   Knockouts: 37

By the time Muhammad Ali retired from the ring, many boxing experts thought he was the best heavyweight champion of all. He earned that the hard way. Even beating the feared Sonny Liston twice when he was still going by the name Cassius Clay, Ali wasn't really taken seriously by the experts. But as he began to pile up wins after wins, and they saw that he had the fastest hands and feet the heavyweight division had ever seen, they began to say maybe he could have licked the great champions like Dempsey and Louis.

Ali bewildered his opponent by doing the unexpected. He never really hurt anyone; a lot of his kayos were cut eyes and TKO variety.

Always a fighter who liked to talk and brag on himself, Ali was never modest. Before a fight he would always have something to say about his opponent or how he was going to whip him. He was great with his ticket-selling abilities.

As a youngster he got involved in boxing in 1954, at the age of twelve. His bike had been stolen from him, and he was sent to an Irish policeman named Joe Martin, who also ran a boxing program for youth. With Martin prodding him on, Ali got serious about the fight game.

As an amateur of eighteen fresh out of Louisville, Ali knew where he was going. He said he was going to the Rome Olympics and win a gold medal and come back and become the greatest heavyweight champion of the world and be the greatest.

As Cassius Clay he won 108 amateur fights and lost only eight. He won two national AAU titles and two national Golden Gloves championship. He breezed through the 1960 Olympics winning a gold medal as a light heavyweight and impressed the nation, not only with his blinding speed and boxing ability but his personality as well.

After the Olympics he came home to Louisville a hero. With the gold medal, he had something to launch him in the professional game.

He soon signed up with a group of twelve area businessmen who gave him a modest week's pay, took care of his taxes, saying they did not want Clay to end up in tax trouble like Joe Louis. When he turned pro in 1960, he turned into a full-blown heavyweight.

Ali had his first pro fight on October 29, 1960, against Tunney Hunsaker, where he won a six-round decision.

Ali was very successful, quickly, running off nineteen straight victories in less than four years. He was very sure of himself in all of his fights. Before he would fight for the title, he had twenty straight victories.

Starting out he made a fast name for himself, getting quick attention with how he dealt with the media. He would tell everyone he was the greatest, then he was the prettiest, then reciting poetry and naming the round in which he would stop his opponent. All this helped make him famous and sell tickets before and after he became champion.

Many people didn't take Ali too seriously in the beginning. Then most of his predictions were coming true. He said he would beat Archie Moore in four, and he did; said he would beat Henry Cooper in five, and he beat him in five. With the win over Archie Moore in 1962, sportswriters began taking Ali seriously.

He proved to be great at predicting the outcome of a fight well ahead of time. By his predicting and winning, he soon found himself the only man capable of giving champion Charles "Sonny" Liston an interesting fight. Liston, a frightful puncher, appeared invincible.

Sonny Liston and Ali signed to fight on February 25, 1964. The odds on the day of the fight were that Clay might not even show up, and if he did, Liston was 8-1 to win. But Clay (Ali) had his own opinion. He said if I don't beat Liston in seven, I won't go to heaven.

Clay came in the ring in very good condition — six feet three, 210 pounds; and twenty-two years old who, despite his size, could whirl dizzily around the ring, stopping only long enough to land pinpoint combination. Clay cut up, wore out Sonny Liston, who couldn't or wouldn't answer the bell for the seventh round. Once again Clay was correct on his prediction.

After winning the championship from Sonny Liston, Cassius Clay announced that he had become a member of the Black Muslim faith, that he had bestowed upon himself a holy name and wished, thereafter, to be known as Muhammad Ali.

Most of the newspapers made a joke of it. They advised him to be a credit to his race the way Joe Louis was. The difference was Joe Louis had to prove himself to white sportswriters to break a color line. But the new Muhammad Ali was not to be budged. He did not listen.

Ali and Liston had their rematch on May 25, 1965. The rematch with Liston was one of the most controversial fights in heavyweight history.

In the very first round, Ali landed a right that knocked Liston down. As Liston was down, Ali stood over him telling him to get up and taunting him. Ali didn't go to a neutral corner, but the timekeeper had started counting. Referee Jersey Joe Walcott didn't start the count but was telling Ali to go to a neutral corner. Liston finally got up as the timekeeper's count reached twenty-two. As Ali and Liston started to fight again, Walcott was told by Nat Fleischer that the fight was over and Ali had won. Walcott stopped the fight, and Ali had won by a first-round knockout.

After the second Liston fight, Ali's second defense of his title was against former champion Floyd Patterson on November 22, 1965. This was a heated fight before it started. Patterson would not call Ali by his new name, instead calling him Cassius Clay. Ali would call Patterson the rabbit, because a rabbit is scale, and also calling him an Uncle Tom, because he went against his religion. Ali said that he was going to punish Patterson and carry the fight. Ali did exactly as he said and punished Patterson for twelve rounds although he could have ended it sooner. It finally ended in round twelve with a knockout. This was the cruelest fight seen from Ali.

Ali soon started to have trouble with the military. He had failed two intelligence tests and was classified 1-Y. Soon his local draft board reclassified him as 1-A. Ali said that he couldn't go into the service because he was a Muslim minister. With a lot of people upset with him over the military problem that he was having in the United States, Ali started to fight overseas in 1966. He soon defeated George Chuvalo in Canada on points and Henry Cooper, again, in England in six rounds. He beat Brian London in England in three rounds and then Karl Mildenberger in Germany in twelve rounds.

Ali fought Ernie Terrell on February 6, 1967. This was his eighth defense of his title. Terrell was bigger and taller than Ali, and many thought that this would be his toughest fight since winning the title. This was a big fight because, like a lot of so-called champions before him, Terrell was the World Boxing Association champion. They had taken that part of the championship from Ali when he said that he had joined the Nation of Islam.

Just like Floyd Patterson, Terrell refused to call Ali by his name and instead called him Clay. This upset Ali big-time, saying that Terrell was calling him by his slave name and that Terrell was an Uncle Tom. The fight was for fifteen rounds. Ali said that a knockout was too good for Terrell and that he wanted to punish and to torture him. He said that he wanted to hit him, give him a spanking, and would continue to ask him, "What's my name?" until Terrell said Ali.

The fight went fifteen rounds as Ali had said. Terrell took a savage and brutal beating. He was almost helpless. Throughout the fight when Ali would land blows, he would call him Uncle Tom. On other times he would shout "What's my name" in an effort to get Terrell to say his name in the ring. After the fight, Terrell had to go to the hospital for emergency surgery. Some of his injuries included a fracture under his left eye and swell of the left retina. Ali unified the heavyweight division, having only one undisputed champion, with this win. Ali defended his title nine times from 1965-67. His last title defense was a knockout victory over veteran contender Zora Folley on March 22, 1967.

Many boxing experts believed that the Ali of 1964 through 1967 is rated up there with Louis, Dempsey, and Marciano. Many think that he could have whipped all three of them. The young Ali of that time could glide into the ring, duck punches with a tiny jerk of his head, land his accurate jabs and crisp combinations, zipper backward, and then start over again.

Ali refused induction into the army in 1967 on the grounds that as a Muslim, he was a conscientious objector. Ali said that his religion would not permit him to fight in a war. This grew waves with veterans' groups and some politicians. At the induction center in Houston, Texas, in 1967, he refused to take the traditional one-step forward.

He was rapidly convicted by a Houston jury of violating the draft law, fined ten thousand dollars; sentenced to five years in prison, the maximum punishment; and lost his boxing license. Ali and his attorney appealed, and he remained free on a five-thousand-dollar bond.

Ali was forced to lay off for three years while his case travelled all the way to the Supreme Court. There he won his case! During this time while being stripped of his title and fighting his case in court, his income consisted of mostly speaking engagements at college campuses. Magazines like *Ebony* and *Jet* kept his name in the limelight.

It bugged a lot of people to think that he was throwing it all away because he wanted to fight for such things as equality for his people. No one has the right to knock a man who fights for the things that he believes in. When they took his title, he lost his prime years, the years between twenty-five and twenty-eight.

When it was okay for Ali to fight again, he was twenty-eight years old. His legs were heavier, and his body had thickened out. No more would he be able to flit about the ring at top speed; no more would we see the vintage Ali. His talents were still so considerable that he was able to win back the heavyweight title twice.

While in exile from the ring for three years, Philadelphia's wicked-hooking Joe Frazier had succeeded Ali. He had to work his way up to a fight with the so-called champion Joe Frazier. To get to Frazier, Ali had to beat two top contenders, the first being

Jerry Quarry. Ali got rid of Quarry by cutting him up so badly that he won by a TKO in three rounds.

Oscar Bonavena—a strong, brute fighter—came next. Bonavena landed hard blows that hurt Ali. Ali knocked Bonavena down three times in the fifteenth round to win by a TKO. With the two wins over Quarry and Bonavena, the chance to fight Frazier was set.

The Frazier and Ali fight took place on March 8, 1971. They fought fifteen bruising rounds. Frazier won on points and also knocked Ali down in the fifteenth round. After losing the championship fight to Frazier, Ali had to wait for another shot at the title. From 1971 to 1973, he fought nine times and won each one.

Ali stayed the number one contender for the title until he met a strong, well-conditioned, ex-marine named Ken Norton. Ali and Norton fought in 1973. At the time, Nortin was not a well-known fighter but a ranked fighter. Norton broke Ali's jaw in the first round. Ali fought all twelve rounds in pain from his jaw because he refused to be TKO'd by Norton. Not being able to fight his fight, Ali lost the twelve-round decision to Norton. Also in 1973, Frazier lost the title to a muscular, hard-hitting fighter named George Foreman.

Six months after losing to Norton, they had a rematch. The second fight was just like the first, a hard-fought fight. Ali had to use all of the ring experience that he had to win the decision over Norton. After the win over Norton, Ali wanted Joe Frazier, the only other fighter to beat him.

The fight with Frazier took place on January 28, 1974. This time Ali fought a smart fight in which he boxed Frazier and stayed off the ropes this time. He got the twelve-round decision over Frazier. This win set him up with a title fight with George Foreman.

On October 30, 1974, George Foreman decided to defend his title against Ali. Ali was a big 14-5 underdog against Foreman, just as he was a heavy underdog against Sonny Liston ten years before in 1964. At the time Ali fought Foreman, Foreman had crushed heavyweight fighters without breaking a sweat. Experts wondered what could Ali possibly do against the twenty-six-year-old Foreman. He was younger and stronger. Ali had a plan to beat Foreman and said that he would dance all night. Most people didn't believe Ali; the experts figured that Foreman would cut off half of the dance floor. Ali tried to make writers believe that Foreman could be beaten. He finally said once and for all why Foreman wasn't such a scary dude by saying, "White folks are more afraid of black folks than black folks is of black folks."

In the end Ali proved to be correct. He used his ring experience and came up with something he called "rope a dope," which consisted of letting Foreman throw ponderous blows at him while he covered up along the ropes, hoping Foreman would tire himself out. Before this fight Foreman was knocking everybody out in the first few rounds. Ali figured to let him tire himself out and get him later. Ali's strategy worked perfectly; Foreman was exhausted by the fourth round.

In the eighth round, Ali landed a hard right that hurt Foreman. Ali pursued him around the ring, landing more haymakers that put Foreman down-and-out for the count. By winning the title back for a second time, he became the second only heavyweight champion to win it again after losing the title. The first champion to do so was Floyd Patterson in 1960.

On September 30, 1 975, Ali fought archrival Joe Frazier. They had fought two previous times with each winning once. This would be their third and final fight with each other. Ali had to survive frightening early rounds of body bearing and rebounded to beat Frazier in a fourteenth-round TKO. Ali would later say that this last fight with Frazier was the hardest, deadliest, and most vicious fight that he had ever had in life. Some would say that this was Ali's last good fight. Later he would be capable of some boring fights. From the time Ali won the title from George Foreman in 1973, he had successfully defended his title ten times.

Ali had his eleventh title defense on February 1 5, 1978, against Leon Spinks. Spinks was the 1976 Olympics light-heavyweight gold medalist. In the fight Spinks slipped Ali's jabs and worked him over inside with two hands. Each time that it appeared as if Ali might be coming on, Spinks would blast him back into the ropes. Spinks won the decision and the title.

After losing the title to Spinks, everybody wanted Ali to retire, figuring that he was too old. Ali refused to listen and fought a rematch with Spinks seven months later. This time he gave the youngster a sound, one-sided boxing lesson. He became the first man in heavyweight history to win the title three times.

Ali retired from the ring in 1978 after winning the title back from Leon Spinks. He stayed retired for only two years, returning to fight the current champion, Larry Holmes, on October 2, 1980. The hunger for the ring, still thinking that he still had it or for the love of money, enticed Ali to try to make another comeback as did other former champions.

Ali, at the age of thirty-eight years old, fought Larry Holmes for the championship. It didn't take long in the fight to know that Ali should not have come back. After the first round, Ali didn't land a punch. Ali could only get off a few punches that didn't mean anything. Holmes, who was one of Ali's sparring partners, went as easy as he could on Ali out of respect for him. The fight had gone ten rounds, and Ali hadn't won a round. He didn't come close. Many times he could have been hurt if Holmes hadn't been merciful, pulling punches that might have inflicted worse pain. Ali's manager stopped the fight in the tenth round. Out of sixty-one fights, the loss to Holmes would be the only time that Ali had been knocked out.

Ali had his last comeback fight on December 11, 1981, against Trevor Berbick. Ali was overweight for the fight, and Berbick won an easy decision. After the fight Ali admitted that he was slow, weak, and at forty, too old to continue to fight. He knew that this was the time to retire.

Losing his last two fights so badly to Holmes and Berbick did not affect what people thought of Ali as a fighter. They knew that he had stayed in the ring too long but haven't forgotten what he had done in the ring and for boxing.

Like Joe Louis, Ali had defeated a lot of former champions. He defeated two light-heavyweight champions—Archie Moore in 1962 and Bob Foster in 1972. He defeated five former heavyweight champions—Sonny Liston in 1964 and again in 1965, Floyd Patterson in 1965 and again in 1972, Joe Frazier in 1974 and again in 1975, George Foreman in 1974, and Leon Spinks in 1978. The only former world champion that Ali did not beat was Larry Holmes.

In 1984 Ali was diagnosed with Parkinson's disease. During his reign as heavyweight champion, Ali was known and loved worldwide. After his retirement from the ring, Ali has become a businessman, a spokesman, and a statesman. He spends a lot of time traveling the globe, giving inspiration to generations of fans despite suffering from Parkinson's disease. Muhammad Ali is still a very popular and famous man unlike a lot of former champions.

Title Vacant: April 28, 1968-February 16, 1970

The fourth title vacant happened in 1968 when Muhammad Ali was stripped of his title for refusing induction into the U.S. Army.

During the year 1970, the heavyweight division had two champions, Jimmy Ellis and Joe Frazier. It was decided that Ellis and Frazier should fight each other on February 16, 1970, to have one true champion. Joe Frazier won the fight with Ellis to become the new heavyweight champion of the world.

Joe Frazier

Joe relaxes with trainer, manager, and confidant Yancey Durham, the man who has guided his boxing career since Frazier first stepped into a ring as an amateur. There's almost a father-son relationship between the two, and it has proven to be one of the longest lasting and most profitable in boxing history. Yank found Joe in a Philadelphia gym.

Frazier bangs a hard right to the head of Buster Mathis during 1968 bout. Joe knocked Mathis out in the eleventh round, avenging his only amateur defeat, when Buster whipped Joe to earn the heavyweight spot on the 1964 U.S. Olympic boxing team. Joe fought as alternate.

Joe Frazier will go down as one of the most determined champions of all time. Smokin' Joe held the heavyweight title from 1970 until 1974.

Joe Frazier poses in a classical boxing style. Once in action, Joe rarely assumes this form, preferring instead to fight from a modified crouch, moving from side to side while always stalking his man.

Oscar Bonavena crashes a hard right smack on Joe's jaw. Bonavena represented more trouble for Frazier than any other opponent, knocking Joe to the canvas twice during the second round of their battle in New York. Frazier never came closer to losing than he did this bout. He managed to get a split decision, but many people disputed the verdict, and the Madison Square Garden crowd booed derisively.

Frazier lands patented left hook to the side of George Chuvalo's face, snaking the punch around the Canadian's right-hand guard. Joe badly mauled Chuvalo in the July 1967 fight, and referee Johnny Colon was forced to stop the scheduled twelve rounder early in the fourth, by which time Chuvalo had already been battered into a gory mess. Frazier was twenty-three years old when he met the Canadian champion.

Joe Frazier is about to move in for the kill in round five of his bout with Jeff Davis who had just gotten up from the floor, but the referee mercifully intervened and awarded the bout to Frazier.

Muhammad Ali vs. Joe Frazier, March 8, 1971: Round one . . .

191

Frazier Knocks Out Mathis in eleventh round of title fight.

COLORED BUSTER MATHIS lies on the bottom rope of the Madison Square ...

Frazier gains undisputed heavyweight title, stopping Ellis in fifth round.

And its effect: Ellis is glassy-eyed as referee Tony Perez counts six. Ellis wobbled to his feet at nine. Frazier is in neutral corner at rear.

Final blow: Joe Frazier landing a right on Jimmy Ellis's jaw in the fourth round of the title fight last night

Joe Frazier

Born: 1944, South Carolina
Weight: 205 lbs., 5'11"
Champion: 1970-1973

Won: 32   Lost: 4   Drew: 1   Knockouts: 27

Joe Frazier will go down as the champion who took the longest time to be considered as the champion of the world. Frazier was a flat-footed slugger with stamina, a devastating puncher, excellent body puncher, and had one of the best left hooks in the history of the heavyweight division. He was always the aggressor, always coming at you, bobbing and weaving and throwing hard punches. Being so relentless as a fighter and coming at his opponent, he would be willing to be hit two or three times to land one of his and all the time never giving his opponent time to breathe in any rounds. At five feet eleven tall, he was short for a heavyweight, but he always fought in fights where height didn't matter anyway. Being well built, strong, and a hard-hitter, Frazier would always battle you for the entire three minutes of each round, putting pressure on you.

Born in South Carolina in 1944, Frazier started boxing at the age of nine when he made a punching bag out of moss and leaves. At sixteen Frazier had moved to Philadelphia. Growing up as a teenager, he was always big and overweight. He would go into the gym to lose weight and discovered that he had punching power.

It was also at the Philadelphia gyms that he was discovered by Yancey Durham. Durham trained and managed Frazier through his amateur and professional career up till he died in 1973.

Fighting out of Philadelphia as an amateur, Frazier won the Golden Gloves in 1962, 1963, and 1964. He then set his mind on the 1964 Olympics. As an amateur, Frazier only lost to Buster Mathis, and this was during the trails for the U.S. Olympics boxing team. When Mathis hurt his hand and couldn't go, Frazier filled in as a substitute. He went on and won a gold medal as a heavyweight in the 1964 Olympics.

After winning his gold medal, Frazier turns pro in 1965. He was sponsored by a Philadelphia group named Cloverlay, Inc. He had his first fight on August 16, 1965; he would win four straight fights, all by knockouts inside of three rounds.

By the end of 1965, his manager Durham knew he had a special fighter in Frazier and a potential heavyweight champion. Durham would hire Eddie Futch, one of the best trainers in boxing, to be Frazier's trainer in 1966. It would be Futch who teaches Frazier to bob and weave to make it harder for his opponents to hit him.

In Frazier's second year as a pro fighter, he fought often with nine fights. He would win all of them, eight by knockouts. Frazier had won ten straight fights by knockout. When he fought Oscar Bonavena in 1966, this would be his toughest opponent before he became champion. During this fight Frazier had to get up off the floor two times in the second round after being floored by Bonavena. He managed to win a split decision over Bonavena that many people didn't agree with.

In 1967 Frazier fought a contender in George Chuvalo, whom he beat in four rounds. By now in 1967, Frazier was a top contender. As he was climbing the ladder to be the number one contender, wearing his opponent down with body blows and finishing them with his deadly left hook, the heavyweight division had no champion in 1967. Muhammad Ali got stripped of his title and was unable to fight anymore.

The WBA sponsored a tournament to find a successor to the title. Frazier was held back by his cornermen to participate in the tournament. This tournament was won by Jimmy Ellis on April 27, 1968, by beating Jerry Quarry by a decision.

The heavyweight division became confusing when the New York Boxing Commission decided that the winner of the match between Joe Frazier and Buster Mathis would be the world champion. In the fight Frazier knocked out Mathis in the eleventh round; by beating Mathis, Frazier was now recognized as champion in New York, five other states, and a couple of countries.

He now shares the title of world heavyweight champion with Jimmy Ellis, who had all of the other states. To me it is best to say that the title was vacant from 1967 until Frazier and Ellis fought in 1970. From 1968 to 1970, there were two champions.

The fight that everyone wanted to see for the undisputed heavyweight title between Frazier and Jimmy Ellis took place on February 16, 1970. In the first round, Ellis looked good in winning the first round. After the first round, it was all Frazier as he took over, landing power punches and applying heavy pressure. In the fourth round, he knocked Ellis down two times from left hooks. Ellis's manager Angelo Dundee, seeing what beating Ellis had taken in the fourth round, stopped the fight, before Ellis could take any more beating, to start round five.

On Frazier's first title defense, he fought Bob Foster, the light-heavyweight champion on November 18, 1970. The fight lasted only two rounds as Foster was much too light and Frazier was much too big and strong for Foster.

In all Frazier would defend his title four times, all wins including a return match with Oscar Bonavena, which he won by a fifteen-round unanimous decision.

Even after beating Jimmy Ellis to become the undisputed heavyweight champion, Frazier never got the recognition he wanted or got the respect he deserved as champion. With Muhammad Ali still undefeated as champion, he was still looked upon by many boxing fans to be the real undefeated champion. Frazier knew to get the recognition he wanted, he had to fight and defeat Ali.

Muhammad Ali got licensed to fight in 1970 and won his two fights against Jerry Quarry and Oscar Bonavena. With these two wins by Ali, Frazier signed to fight Ali on March 8, 1971.

Just like the Frazier and Ellis fight, the Frazier and Ali fight was the fight everybody wanted to see, even more so with the two champions being undefeated. They fought fifteen hard, bruising rounds; Frazier never gave Ali any breathing room from the start to finish. Frazier had Ali staggering in the eleventh round, seemingly ready to go. Toward the end of the fifteenth round, Frazier landed a powerful left hook, sending Ali to the canvas, only to see Ali get right back up. At the end of the fight, Frazier had won a unanimous decision over Ali. The fight was so brutal that both fighters had to spend some time at the hospital.

After beating Ali in 1971, Frazier had three more title defenses. Two in 1972 with a four-round win over Terry Daniels on January 15, and on May 25 with a win over Ron Stander.

On January 22, 1973, Frazier had the third defense of his title, this time against George Foreman. Going into the fight, Frazier was undefeated at 29-0 and a 3-1 favorite to win.

In the fight with Foreman, Frazier's style of fighting would hurt him and benefit Foreman. He kept coming at Foreman, Foreman being the much harder puncher and a bigger fighter. Foreman met him, applying pressure to Frazier. Foreman didn't have to find Frazier, and he never backed up. Foreman floored Frazier three times in the first round and three more times in the second round when the fight was stopped.

With the loss of his title to Foreman, Frazier wanted his title back. He would have a win over Joe Bugner and then a rematch with Muhammad Ali. Unlike their first fight, neither Frazier nor Ali was champion. This time Ali won by a unanimous decision.

Now with two losses, Frazier was still on the comeback trail. He would have two wins over two contenders. On June 17, 1974, Frazier won a rematch with Jerry Quarry, winning by a knockout of Quarry in five rounds. On March 2, 1975, he would have a rematch with Jimmy Ellis, winning in nine rounds over Ellis. Now with these two wins, he was now top contender to fight the new champion Muhammad Ali who had beaten George Foreman for the title in 1974.

Frazier would fight for the title for the last time against Muhammad Ali on October 1, 1975. Like their other two fights, it was a very hard-fought fight, very brutal; and both fighters took a bad beating. Ali won the fight after Frazier cornerman Eddie Futch thought that Frazier had taken a beating in round fourteen and threw out the fight. Futch would not let Frazier come out for the fifteenth round.

Still not finish, Frazier would fight a rematch with George Foreman on June 15, 1976. This time Foreman knocks Frazier out in five rounds. With this loss to Foreman, Frazier retired from the ring.

Being out of the ring for almost five years, he would make a comeback to the ring on December 3, 1981. Frazier fought Floyd (Jumbo) Cummings. Both fighters were way overweight, and they fought a ten-round draw. This would be Frazier's last fight.

Frazier would go down as one of the hardest-hitting champions ever. He won 73 percent of his fights by knockout and is in the Boxing Hall of Fame. Muhammad Ali would say that his third fight with Frazier was his toughest championship fight.

After Frazier's boxing career was over, he went on the entertaining route, singing; and he managed his son Marvis Frazier to a heavyweight title fight with the champion Larry Holmes; Frazier spends a lot of his time in the gym he owns, managing it in Philadelphia, grooming future boxers.

George Foreman

Foreman succeeded Frazier as the Olympic kingpin in 1968.

Foreman, who idolized former champion Sonny Liston, continued his destruction of top-rated heavyweights with a second-round demolition of Ken Norton.

In 1973, Foreman upset champion Joe Frazier in Kingston, Jamaica, to win the title. He dropped Frazier six times en route to a second-round kayo.

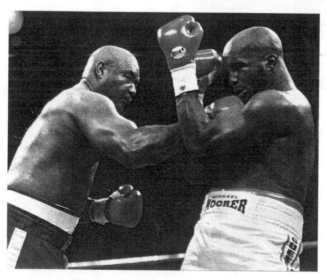

Foreman's right hand launches him to new heights.

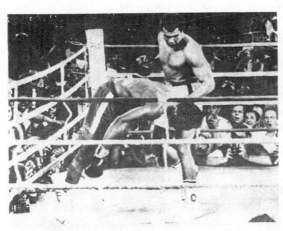

Stunning disbelievers, Ali pulled rope-a-dope trick out of his bag and took the title away from George Foreman in 1974.

George Foreman was, without question, the most awesome slugger in heavyweight history.

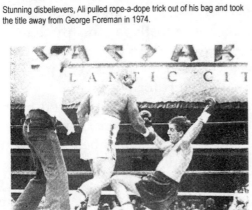

After a ten-year retirement, a much heavier Foreman launched a comeback in 1987. But it wasn't until his second-round destruction of former contender Gerry Cooney in January 1990 that he was taken seriously.

Foreman towers over a floored Tony Fulilangi, who departed in just two rounds.

George Foreman

Born: 1948, Texas
Weight: 224 lbs., 6'3"
Champion: 1973-1974, 1994-1995

Wins: 76   Lost: 5   Draws: 0   Knockouts: 69

Many boxing experts think that George Foreman was the hardest hitter in heavyweight history, by far the most devastating puncher since Joe Louis. He won twenty-four consecutive fights by knockouts before he lost the title. One time in his career, he had won forty straight fights, thirty-seven by knockouts.

George was strictly a puncher, mostly a one puncher. It usually didn't take but one punch. He didn't do much moving and no running. Foreman was very strong and a very powerful hitter. When he hit you, you would hurt for weeks.

Growing up in Houston, Texas, Foreman was raised by his mother. He spent a lot of time getting into trouble. He would beat up and rob people on the street. He would also beat up kids in school. He quit school in the ninth grade.

Later in 1965, Foreman signed up for the Job Corps hoping to learn a trade. Even in the Job Corps, he was getting into fights. It was there, since he was so big and fast, that he was persuaded to try boxing and to learn how to box. In the Job Corp, he won trophies and fought in the Golden Gloves competition. He graduated in 1967.

In 1 967 Foreman won the national AAU heavyweight title. He then set out to fight in the 1968 Olympics where he won a gold medal in the heavyweight division. With the gold medal now, Foreman wanted to turn pro and make big money for his mother and family.

Foreman turned pro in 1969. He had his first professional fight on June 23, 1969, against Don Waldheim, whom he knocked out in the third round. From the start he looked like a championship prospect with a lethal right hand. After winning his first fight, Foreman won a total of thirty-seven straight fights, thirty-four by knockouts. Foreman now figured that he was ready to challenge the champion, Joe Frazier.

Frazier and Foreman signed to fight on January 22, 1973. The Foreman and Frazier fight was a fight between two knockout artists. The only way the two could fight was toe-to-toe. Frazier wears his man down with body attack and Foreman, a lot of times, with just one punch.

Even with Foreman's great record, it was not thought that he could beat Frazier. Frazier was 3-1 favorite to win, and many people said that Foreman hadn't really beaten anyone in his thirty-seven wins.

Little did they know, Foreman destroyed the feared Frazier in two rounds. Foreman had knocked Frazier down six times before referee Arthur Merecante stopped the match in the second round.

After winning the title from Frazier, Foreman had two successful title defenses. He knocked out Jose "King" Roman in one round and then defeated the number one contender Ken Norton in two rounds.

By Foreman destroying Ken Norton in two rounds and also having already destroyed Frazier in two rounds, he was now looked upon by boxing fans to be an absolute terror and feared in the ring. There were people who thought he'd be champion for as long as he cared to be. Foreman could cut off the floor on any opponent. There was no way to escape his devastating blows. Everything was going pretty well for him in the ring, winning nearly all of his fights in the early rounds. Foreman's third title defense came on October 30, 1974.

This fight was against Muhammad Ali, and Foreman was a 3-1 favorite to win. Foreman's plan was to cut off the ring on Ali. In the early rounds, Ali lay on the ropes, while Foreman wailed away with both hands and did not really land any of them. By the fourth round, Foreman was beginning to become tired from throwing so many punches. As Foreman was punching himself out, his punches were getting weaker and weaker. Ali saw this and began to take charge of the fight instead of being on the defense.

Ali started to throw more jabs and hard rights to Foreman's head, which took effect. Ali knocked Foreman out in the eighth round. Foreman lost his title to Ali because he had punched himself out, he had trouble fighting into the later rounds of the fight, and because of Ali's ring experience.

Foreman, in trying to get a rematch with Ali, ran off a list of knockouts. They were against opponents like Joe Frazier, Ron Lyle, and Scott LeDoux. These matches were against sluggers, not boxers. The boxing fans still did not know what to expect from Foreman.

A lot was answered about Foreman when he fought his last fight with Jimmy Young on March 17, 1977. In the seventh round, he had Young hurt from a solid left hook but seemed too fatigued to put his opponent out. Young later admitted that Foreman could have put him away in the seventh round. In the final round, Young put the tired Foreman down for the count. Young won a unanimous twelve-round decision. Foreman looked exhausted and spent the night in the hospital.

The next day sitting up in his hospital bed, Foreman said that he was retiring from the ring to devote his life to God. At the time of his statement, he had a record of forty-five wins, two losses, and forty-five knockouts. Many people said that Foreman was using religion as an excuse for losing to Jimmy Young. Foreman was for real. He would become a pastor, an evangelist, and even have his own church.

While being retired from the ring, Foreman also started the George Foreman Youth and Community Center. He paid for everything, the mortgage, equipment, utilities, and maintenance. After being retired for ten years and money getting low, Foreman decided to make a comeback in 1987 saying, "Fighting is a lot more important to me this time." While boxing again, he would continue to preach and run his community center.

From 1987 to 1991, Foreman had twenty-four fights, winning all of them, and twenty-three by knockouts. Twenty-three of his fights were against journeymen. Adilson Rodriques, whom he knocked out in the second round, was the only ranked contender. These twenty-four wins earned Foreman a title fight, at age forty-two, with the champion Evander Holyfield. The fight took place on April 19, 1991, went the distance with Holyfield winning a unanimous twelve-round decision.

In Foreman's return to the ring, he has fought as light as 235 lbs. but has mostly fought with a weight of between 250-260 lbs. He is old, in his forties, slow, and needs mostly a stationary target. Foreman uses a "crossed arm in front of the face" defense at this stage in his career. The punching power has not gone anywhere; it's still the same, winning by early rounds knockouts.

Foreman, still hoping for another title fight, signed to fight Alex Stewart in April 1992. It is in this fight that Foreman took one of the worst beatings in both of his boxing careers. Foreman was able to win a very close decision only because he scored two knockdowns in the second round. Foreman suffered, both eyes were nearly shut, and his whole face was swollen. Many boxing fans wanted Foreman to finally retire again.

After getting beaten up so badly, but still able to win, Foreman came back, in his next fight, to beat Pierre Coetzer. He won this fight in an eighth-round knockout. Foreman had another setback on June 7, 1993. At the age of forty-four, he lost a one-sided unanimous decision to Tommy Morrison.

In 1994, Foreman was offered to fight for the title held by Michael Moorer, who had beaten Evander Holyfield for the title. At the time Foreman was forty-five years old. On his comeback of seven years, his record was twenty-seven wins and two losses. The fight was to take place on November 5, 1994, for the heavyweight championship.

In the fight Moorer was landing a lot of punches, winning all of the rounds and hurting Foreman. By the ninth round, Moorer was way ahead on points, and only a knockout would win the fight.

In the tenth round, Foreman hit Moore with a hard right to the head that knocked him down and out! Foreman was the world heavyweight champion again, twenty years after beating Joe Frazier for the title.

Foreman would later get stripped of his title in 1995 for not fighting the number one contender. He would win a couple of more fights in the ring and had his last fight in 1997 against Shannon Briggs. Briggs won by a twelve-round decision. In his last fight against Briggs, Foreman was forty-eight years old.

From all of the many accomplishments in his career (winning the gold medal at the Olympics and winning the heavyweight title twice), maybe the biggest accomplishment was the comeback journey that he started in 1987 after being retired for ten years. He has earned over twenty-seven million dollars during his comeback to the ring. He is partnered with George Foreman Grill, a successful businessman, and continues to do God's work. Foreman retired from the ring in 1997. Out of the greatest one hundred power punchers, he is at nine. He was inducted into the International Boxing Hall of Fame in 2003.

Leon Spinks

After 1976 Olympics, Mrs. Spinks joins sons, Michael (l) and Leon, who won gold medals carrying the banner of the United States.

Spinks first gained stardom when he won a gold medal at the 1976 Olympics. Less than two years later, he outpointed Muhammad Ali to win the heavyweight title.

The fifteenth was wicked. Ali drives Spinks into the ropes (l), but Spinks comes back to tag Ali, a tired champion.

Flashing the now-famous gaping smile, Spinks glories as the new champion.

Leon Spinks (right), light-heavyweight gold medalist of the Montreal Olympics, St. Louis, connects with a hard left to the midsection of "Lightning" Bob Smith in Los Angeles during the Las Vegas bout. (Above) Spinks finishes off Smith in the fifth round.

Spinks's "victory" didn't help his image.

Leon Spinks

Born: 1953, Missouri
Weight: 200 lbs., 6'1"
Champion: 1978-1978

Won: 26   Lost: 17   Drew: 3   Knockout: 14

Leon Spinks was very hard to figure as a champion. He came and went before any boxing fan had a chance to realize who or what was. As a fighter, he fought in an awkward style.

Leon started his amateur career in 1974. He won the AAU light-heavyweight championship in 1974, 1975, and 1976. In 1976 Olympics, Spinks won a gold medal as a light heavyweight.

In 1977 Leon turned pro and had his first professional fight on January 15, 1977, against Bob Smith, whom he knocked out in five rounds. He would go on and win his first five fights in 1977, all by knockouts.

With only seven professional fights, Leon was signed to fight the champion Muhammad Ali for the title on February 15, 1978. At the time, Leon had a record of six wins and one draw with Scott LeDoux.

In the championship fight with Ali, Leon was a big 8-1 underdog in this fight. From the time the fight started, Leon was relentless and kept the pressure on Ali, giving him no breathing room, and pounded Ali throughout the fight in the corners. Leon never tired in the fight, fought the late rounds like the early rounds, while winning the decision and the title over Ali.

As the champion he never wore the celebrity status; instead he was constantly in trouble with the law. After beating Ali, Leon would never, for the rest of his career, fight that good.

The rematch with Ali happened on September 15, 1978. The rematch would be different because Ali, unlike in the first fight, trained hard to get his title back, and Leon didn't. The seven months leading up to the rematch with Ali, Leon was an undisciplined fighter in training. While he was training to fight Ali, Leon was drinking alcohol, doing dope, and getting into trouble with the law.

In the rematch Leon didn't have a chance. Ali stayed in Leon's face the whole fight by using his skills, ring smarts, and jabs. Ali won by a unanimous fifteen-round decision. Ali retired after winning his title back from Leon.

With his title now gone, Leon still wanted to fight. His next fight was a WBA tournament to find a successor. He fought against Gerrie Coetzee on June 24, 1979. Coetzee won by knocking Leon out in the first round.

The year 1980 would be better to Leon. He had won two fights in a row by knockouts—Bernardo Mercado and Evangelista. The win over Bernardo was big because Bernardo was a ranked contender. He earned a shot at the title to fight the champion Larry Holmes because of these two wins.

The championship fight with Larry Holmes happened on June 12, 1981. In this title fight, Leon was no match for Holmes who knocked Leon out in the third round. This would be Leon's last try at the heavyweight title.

Leon moved down a level and started fighting as a cruiserweight after having lost to Holmes. In Leon's first four fights, he won two and lost two. In 1985 Leon had won four straight fights and had earned a shot at the cruiserweight title held by Dwight Qauri on March 26, 1986.

In the fight with Qauri, he was beaten up and taunted for six rounds until the referee stopped it because Leon offered no resistance. This would be his last fight for fighting for any title. Leon would continue to fight but lost much of the time. At one point, Leon had lost seven of nine fights. He retired from the ring in 1988 because of the losses.

Leon was making a comeback to the ring by 1991. He would win some but would lose more. He had an 8-4 record on his comeback trail. One of his losses was against John Carlo on October 22, 1994. What was so bad was that Leon was knocked out in the first round and that it was Carlo's first professional fight.

Leon had the one big fight to win the title from Ali, and then he never gave his career a chance. From the time that he beat

Ali for the title, Leon lived a hard life. He was partying, doing drugs and alcohol, and blowing lots of money. He was never a dedicated fighter. He became bankrupt and homeless.

Leon could have had a much better fighting career if he would have trained and fought like he did for the first Ali fight. He was a very good, aggressive fighter. His career was doomed because of his vices and not training properly.

After his boxing career was over, Leon worked as a bartender and at the YMCA. He was with his son Cory Spinks, a boxer who became the undisputed welterweight champion of the world.

Larry Holmes

Bombarding Kenny Norton's head with blows to gain the WBC championship, Larry Holmes (rt) won a fifteen-round battle, barely earning split decision. Fight was deadlocked going into the last round, which Holmes won handily.

Larry Holmes's most destructive performance may have been his third-round kayo of Leon Spinks in June 1981. Holmes scored stoppages in eleven of his first twelve title defenses, with only Trevor Berbick lasting the distance.

The title fight Larry Holmes had to win was his June 1982 showdown with top-rated contender Gerry Cooney. Holmes, sharp and prepared, boxed brilliantly and halted his foe in the thirteenth round in Las Vegas.

Old age and Tyson bowled Holmes over in '88.

By the fifth round, the rope a dope was utilized more to keep Ali upright than to wear Holmes down.

Larry Holmes

Born: 1949, Georgia
Weight: 212 lbs., 6'3"
Champion: 1978-1985

Won: 69   Lost: 6   Drew: 0   Knockouts: 44

Larry Holmes was known in the ring as a very good and smart fighter. He had one of the best jabs ever in the heavyweight division, punching power and good movement. Like Joe Louis, Holmes was a fighting champion who fought everyone.

The Holmes's family moved from Georgia to Easton, Pennsylvania, in 1954. It was there that Holmes started boxing at the local Pal and Youth Center in Easton.

In 1968 Holmes started fighting as an amateur. He had twenty-two fights, winning nineteen of them. He later became a sparring partner for Muhammad Ali at his training camp in Pennsylvania for years. Holmes learned a lot of his boxing by being Ali's sparring partner. He also was a sparring partner for Joe Frazier.

Holmes turned pro in 1973. He had his first professional fight on March 21, 1973, against Rodell Dupree, whom he beat in four rounds. 1973 would be a busy year for Holmes as he would have seven fights, winning all of them.

From 1973 to 1978, Holmes won all his fights; he kept on winning but getting no respect. He won twenty-six straight fights, twenty by knockouts, but getting not much respect.

When he fought Earnie Shavers on March 25, 1978, and beat Shavers, he got the respect he wanted. The boxing world became aware of Holmes with the win over a top contender like Shavers. He soon was a top-ranked fighter, eventually fighting Ken Norton for the title.

On June 10, 1978, Larry Holmes and Ken Norton fought for the title. In one of the best championship fight ever in a nonstop-action fight, Holmes won a split decision to become the new champion.

Muhammad Ali had retired after winning his title back from Leon Spinks in 1978. With Ali retired as champion, Holmes never got his full credit as champion.

Holmes never got his full credit as champion until Muhammad Ali came out of retirement two years later to fight him on October 2, 1980. The fight was a mismatch as Holmes won all ten rounds from Ali, even holding back because Ali was his idol. Ali failed to come out for round eleven. With Ali gone, he was the true champion. Following Muhammad Ali as champion was not easy to Holmes.

As champion Holmes was greatly compared to former champions. He broke Joe Louis's record with eight straight knockouts in title defense. With this, it helped Holmes to finally get recognized as a true champion. Before his years would be up as champion, Holmes had twenty title defenses. Only Joe Louis with twenty-five had more. Next to Joe Louis, he was the best fighting champion.

Holmes had a scare when he defended his title in a rematch with Earnie Shavers on September 28, 1979. He fought a good fight, scoring almost at will with his jabs round after round. Shavers was having trouble landing his powerful right as Holmes kept moving to his right to keep away from Shavers's powerful right.

Everything was going fine for Holmes until in the seventh round when Shavers landed one of his powerful right's, sending Holmes to the floor. He got up and held and ran for the rest of the round.

Starting the eighth, it was back to the same as Holmes started picking Shavers apart with his jabs. By the eleventh round, Shavers was helpless as Holmes scored at will until the referee stopped the round.

As he continued to beat all challengers, at one point in his boxing career, he was 48-0. Holmes had beaten former champion Leon Spinks in three rounds. The biggest win he had as a champion was a win over number one contender Gerry Cooney in the thirteenth round. That win over Cooney gave him what respect that was left for him to get.

With forty-eight wins and no losses, he wanted to tie Rocky Marciano's record of forty-nine wins and no loss.

Holmes's opponent to tie Marciano's record was Michael Spinks, the light-heavyweight champion on September 22, 1985. Spinks won the fight by a decision. Holmes got a rematch with Spinks but again lost by a decision. After the second loss to Spinks, he retired from the ring.

Holmes made a comeback to the ring to fight the current champion Mike Tyson on January 22, 1988, after being retired from the ring for two years. In the title fight with Tyson, Holmes was far from his prime and got knocked out in the fourth round by Tyson and retired from the ring again. When he lost his title match by a fourth-round knockout to Mike Tyson, it was the first time Holmes had been knocked out in seventy-five professional fights.

Still wanting to fight and go for the championship, Holmes made yet a third comeback to the ring. Being out of the ring for three years, Holmes signed to fight Eddy Gonzales on August 13, 1991. In this fight he beat Gonzales by a ten-round decision.

Holmes would go on and win six straight fights. His biggest win in his comeback was a win over Ray Mercer, who was a top contender to the title. The win over Mercer earned him a title fight with the champion Evander Holyfield.

On June 19, 1992, Holmes got his second championship fight after his first retirement from the ring. In his title fight against Holyfield, he lost a twelve-round decision to Holyfield. For this fight he was forty-two years old.

Holmes had his last fight on July 27, 2002 against Eric "Butterbean" Esch. In this fight Holmes won by a ten-round decision.

Larry Holmes held the title for seven and a half years, successfully defended his title twenty times against any fighter who wanted a title shot. His natural ability was well known. What made him just as great was his great recuperation skill, rising from knockdown in defense of his title against Renaldo Snipes and Earnie Shavers. With his excellent jab and a hard right, he was always constantly moving, and he couldn't be intimidated.

After his boxing career was over, Holmes dealt in different businesses and real estate. He was elected to the Boxing Hall of Fame in 2008.

Michael Spinks

Michael Spinks proudly displays his collection of world championship belts.

Spinks's lefts helped him beat Eddie Mustafa Muhammad for the WBA light-heavyweight crown. Then Spinks beat another Muhammad—Dwight Muhammad Qawi, the WBC champion—to unify the title.

In 1985, Spinks outboxed Larry Holmes to win a unanimous decision and become the first reigning light-heavy champ to capture the heavyweight title.

218

Every fighter remembers the best punch he ever landed, and Spinks is no different. He says his best shot was the big right hand that nailed Russian Rufat Riskiev in the finals of the 1976 Olympics. Riskiev had beaten Spinks in a previous tournament, so Spinks saw the punch as payback.

Gerry Cooney stood no chance against Spinks in their 1987 fight. By the fifth round, Spinks had measured the bigger man and sent him crashing to the canvas, dashing the dreams of yet another white hope.

Mike Tyson sent Spinks into retirement with a first-round knockout in 1988. Even though Spinks was a complete fighter, he'd been off for a year and couldn't get his timing down.

Michael Spinks

Born: 1956, Missouri
Weight: 200 lbs., 6'2"
Champion: 1985-1987

Won: 31   Lost: 1   Draws: 0   Knockout: 21

Michael Spinks was a very gifted fighter, but he may be looked at as a fighter who did much better as a light heavyweight where he dominated that division.

As an amateur Michael had a great record of 93-7; he won the Golden Gloves as a middleweight in 1974 and in 1976. In the 1976 Olympics, he won a gold medal as a middleweight.

Michael turns pro in 1977 fighting as a light heavyweight. In his first professional fight, he fought Eddie Benson on April 17, 1977, whom he knocked out in the first round.

Boxing fans knew who Michael was in 1980 when he had a great year. He had two wins over two top contenders in Murray Sutherland and Alvaro Yaqui Lopez. Then in 1981 he had a four-round victory over another top contender in Marvin Johnson.

With the win over Marvin Johnson and with him winning sixteen straight fights with eleven knockouts and beating all the top contenders, he became the number one contender to fight the light-heavyweight champion Eddie Mustafa Muhammad.

Michael fought for the title against Muhammad on July 18, 1981. The fight was a hard tough fight with Michael knocking Muhammad down in the twelfth round, going on to beating Muhammad for the title.

After winning the light-heavyweight title, Michael had five successful title defensives. Michael's sixth title defense would be his biggest. This would be a fight with Dwight Muhammad Qawi (Dwight Braxton) who was the WBC champion. Michael and

Qawi fought on March 18, 1983, to unify the light-heavyweight title. Michael won a unanimous fifteen-round decision to be the undisputed champion of the world.

Fighting as a light-heavyweight, Michael was very successful, with a perfect 31-0 record. He made ten successful title defenses from 1981 to 1985. At the time that Michael was the champion, the light heavyweight was loaded with good top fighters, but nobody could beat him. He dominated the light-heavyweight division like very few champions had.

By having beaten everyone, there was no more money to be made in the light-heavyweight division. He now wanted to move up and win the heavyweight title. He said he wanted to make history since a lot of good light heavyweight had tried, but all had failed.

By 1984 there were talks to Spinks fighting the heavyweight champion Larry Holmes for the heavyweight title. All the sportswriters said that it was a big mismatch. The same way Spinks had dominated light heavyweight, Holmes had dominated the heavyweight division for years. At this time Holmes was going for Rocky Marciano's perfect record of 49-0.

After beating all the top light-heavyweight contenders and still the light-heavyweight champion, Spinks decided to fight as a heavyweight in 1985. Spinks knew that the heavyweight division at the time was not that strong, and he knew that Larry Holmes was not the same champion he was years ago. He also had sparred with, as a light heavyweight, against heavyweights like Tim Witherspoon, Randy "Tex" Cobb, and Greg Page. Spinks knew that he sparred well with these top contenders, and he knew he was ready to move up in weight to the heavyweight.

On September 22, 1985, Larry Holmes signed to defend his title against Michael Spinks. For this title fight, Spinks was a big underdog because Holmes was a great fighting champion who had beaten all the top heavyweight contenders. Also he was an underdog because a lot of great light-heavyweight champions like Billy Conn, Archie Moore, and Bob Foster had fought for the heavyweight title and lost.

Hearing all this did not discourage Spinks; he thought otherwise. This was not the same Larry Holmes who had destroyed his big brother Leon so bad three years ago in 1981. Holmes had gone downhill.

To set his goal on winning the heavyweight title, he knew he had to fight at a heavyweight weight. He accomplished this with the aid of sports nutritionist Mackie Shilstone. At the weigh-in, Spinks weighed two hundred pounds; with solid muscles he had lost none of his speed and was undefeated in twenty-seven fights.

During the fight with Holmes, the extra weight did not make him sluggish. Spinks fought a smart fight, was able to duck in and out and stay away from Holmes's power. Spinks only went in for certain bursts at a time and constantly confusing Holmes, who looked the thirty-five years of age he was. All through the fight, Holmes's main plan was to land a power punch. The opportunities vanished as soon as they came. In the end Spinks had won unanimous decision.

In doing so Michael Spinks had become the first world light-heavyweight champion to succeed in a bid to become the world heavyweight champion. He had also become the first brother of a former world champ to hold a world title in the same division. Just like his brother Leon in beating Muhammad Ali for the title in 1978, Michael had pulled off one of the greatest upset in heavyweight division. Seven months later in a rematch, he again beat Holmes, this time by a close fifteen-round split decision.

After winning the heavyweight title from Homes, he gave up the light-heavyweight title, fighting only as a heavyweight.

Michael held the title for the next two years. As a heavyweight he didn't have much power, but had success with his speed and awkward movement. Michael had one defense of his title, winning over Steffen Tangstand by a knockout in four rounds. In 1987 Michael was stripped of his title for not fighting the number one contender.

Mike Tyson became the new champion, but some fans still looked at Michael as still the champion. Tyson and Michael fought on June 28, 1988. In the fight Tyson won in ninety-one seconds of the first round. This was Michael's only loss as a professional fighter. In the fight Michael said that Tyson came on him real fast up in his face before he even knew he was there. Instead of fighting his fight, he stood there and tried to fight with Tyson and got knocked out. This was also his last fight, retiring from the ring afterward.

After his retirement from the ring, he would later be elected to the Boxing Hall of Fame and worked with Butch Lewis and Lewis fighters.

Mike Tyson

Tyson throws a right to the face of Tucker during late-round action of the championship fight in Las Vegas. Wearied gladiators, Tucker (l) and Tyson embrace following the twelve-round fight.

Winning by a unanimous decision, Tyson holds heavyweight champion-ship belts signifying his unification of the championship.

Tyson's viciousness was never more evident than during his brutal seventh-round TKO over 1984 Olympic gold medalist Tyrell Biggs. "I was hitting him with punches to the body and he was making noises," Tyson said afterward. "It was somewhat like a woman screaming."

"No one who was at Tyson's demolition of Holmes will ever forget the sound of the short, arcing right hand that sent Holmes down."

In one of the few instances where Tyson had punching room, he clocks Smith with a clubbing hit. When Tyson was able, he did hurt Smith.

Tyson braces himself against the charging Botha.

Tyson's conviction in '92 for raping Desiree Washington (inset) left boxing more sullied than usual.

Much of the controversy surrounding Mike Tyson centered on his wife, Robin Givens (left), and his mother-in-law, Ruth Roper, pictured here at the official weigh-in.

225

Mike Tyson

Born: 1966, New York
Weight: 218 lbs., 5'11"
Champion: 1987-1990

Won: 50   Lost: 6   Draws: 0   Knockouts: 44

Mike Tyson was the most ferocious, intimidating, and dangerous puncher that the heavyweight division had seen since George Foreman reigned (1973-1974). Tyson appeared to have no obstacles in the ring; most of his wins came early in the fights and usually by knockouts.

Mike was raised by his mother after being abandoned by his father early on in life. Mike didn't have it easy growing up in urban Brooklyn, New York. He was surrounded by gangs and crime. He eventually submitted to his surroundings by becoming a gang member and committing various crimes himself. By his early teenage years, Mike had been arrested several times, mostly for stealing, street fighting, and committing armed robbery. During that time, he earned a reputation of being a good fighter. This rough beginning aided his quest to become a major boxing contender.

Because of his repeated mishaps with the law, Mike was sent to a juvenile correctional home for delinquent kids. At the home, there was a guard by the name of Bobby Stewart. Bobby was an ex-boxer and wanted to help Mike channel his aggression into boxing. Mike agreed, and over time, Stewart began to recognize Mike's potential to become a dynamic fighter.

Mike's skills and enthusiasm for boxing generated Bobby to take him to visit Cus D'Amato, the great manager of champions including Floyd Patterson, former heavyweight champion. Cus was so impressed with Mike's boxing ability that he wanted Mike to live with him and train on full-time bases. Cus believed that

Mike had what it took to be a heavyweight champion. The New York State Correction Department granted Tyson permission to stay with Cus. He helped Mike perfect his boxing skills. He taught Mike how to slip a left and counter with a right, how to bob and weave, how to throw a hook, and how to throw a jab. The most important thing he taught the young Tyson was discipline and how to use it in life.

As an amateur, Mike won the Golden Gloves in 1984. He also won the Junior Olympics. During this time in his life, he gained the reputation as a "hard puncher." Many of the managers would not let their young fighters box with Tyson because of that reputation. His cornermen had a hard time recruiting sparring partners for him when training in the gym. Cus had to shell out more money to obtain sparring opponents, even though Tyson was still an amateur and these guys sparred with professional boxers. Out of an estimated fifty-two amateur boxing matches, Tyson lost five (5).

In 1984, Tyson was invited to try out for the 1984 Olympics. He lost two (2) controversial fights in the heavyweight trials to Henry Tillman. He was accepted as an alternate.

Mike turned professional in 1985 and became a sought-after boxer. He entered his professional career as a knockout artist. He had one of the best starting careers in heavyweight boxing history. At nineteen years old, he won fifteen consecutive fights, all by knockout. By the end of 1985, the world had taken notice of Mike Tyson.

The only sad note in 1985 was the death of his manager Cus D'Amato. Cus never witnessed the arrival of his second world heavyweight boxing champion.

As Tyson continued to win, it became apparent that he needed to fight better opponents. He knocked out the first nineteen opponents with only one match going over six rounds. His twentieth match was against James "Quick" Tillie, a more worthy opponent. Tillie went the distance, forcing Tyson to win by decision.

By the time Tyson was twenty-one, no heavyweight had a chance of defeating him. He destroyed every opponent in his path.

Tyson was a very active boxer; he had professionally fought thirty-two times at this point. Out of the thirty-two bouts, twenty-eight were knockouts; twenty of those knockouts occurred in two (2) rounds or less. Never before had a heavyweight boxer achieved that status in such a short time.

Tyson's no-nonsense fighting skills had him delivering devastating punches with either hand. He was well built and loved to stay on the inside of an opponent where his blows were most effective. He hardly broke a sweat kayoing the sad shell of the former heavyweight champion Larry Holmes.

As Tyson continued to win, he became a top contender for the title. In 1986 there were so many so -called world champions, and Tyson went through all of them. First he defeated Trevor Berbick with a single short left that sat Berbick down three (3) times in the most one-sided title bout since Foreman vs. Frazier in 1973. With the Berbick win, Tyson won the World Boxing Council championship belt. He then went on to defeat James "Bonecrusher" Smith by points in a twelve-round bout. This defeat earned him the World Boxing Association title. Tyson won his final title in August 1987 by defeating Tony Tucker in a twelve-round match on points. That win earned him the International Boxing Federation title.

With wins over Berbick, Smith, and Tucker, Tyson achieved the title of undisputed heavyweight champion of the world in 1987. At twenty-one years, two (2) months, and one (1) day old, he was also the youngest heavyweight to win the title. This record beat out Floyd Patterson, the former reigning holder.

Even after unifying the heavyweight division, some boxing fans deemed Michael Spinks the real champion because he had not lost the title in a boxing match. Spinks was in fact stripped of the title for not fighting the number one contender.

Tyson and Spinks finally fought on June 28, 1988. Both fighters were undefeated at the time. Spinks's record was 31-0, and Tyson's was 32-0. Spinks was thirty-one years old at the time, ten years Tyson's senior. Tyson destroyed Spinks in the first round. Tyson again delivered a one-sided, history-making fight. He landed a shattering right hook that put Spinks out in ninety-one seconds. Tyson received twenty-one million, and Spinks received thirteen million for the short fight. That was the most money two boxers had ever made for one match at the same time.

As the reigning champion, Mike was known for his harsh remarks toward his opponents before a match. He would taunt them with comments like "If he's not dead, it won't count" and raved on how he loved to see opponent's blood in the ring. Most disturbing about the comments is that everyone knew that he meant what he said.

Since turning professional at the age of eighteen, Mike remained undefeated for five (5) years. This man smashed every challenger who dare attempted. He even defeated two (2) former champions (Larry Holmes and Michael Spinks) along the way. He also beat Tyrell Biggs, a former Olympic gold medal winner, in four (4) rounds.

Tyson was a controversial fighter. From 1988 he was in controversy, going through a divorce from actress Robin Givens and getting rid of his cornermen Bill Clayton and longtime trainer Kevin Rooney who had been with him from the beginning when Tyson first turned pro. It was Rooney that continued to make Tyson the great fighter that he was after the death of Cus D'Amato in 1985. Now Don King was running the show for Tyson.

With his trainer Kevin Rooney gone now, Tyson wasn't as active a fighter as he was before. In 1989 Tyson had only two fights, an all-time low for him since he turned professional in 1985. These two fights were knockouts over both Frank Bruno and Carl "the Truth" Williams. Also without Rooney in his corner, Tyson became more of a one-big-punch fighter, always headhunting. At first he boxed in the peek-a-boo style, threw combination of punches, and attacked the body. Now he had lost some of his defensive skills, and other skills had gone down.

On February 11, 1990, Tyson fought James "Buster" Douglas. By this time, Tyson was not the same fighter; he didn't have the same training habits, didn't have the same personal life, but was still a very young fighter. Before the fight, Tyson was a huge forty plus to one favorite to win. He took Douglas as a pushover, an easy early knockout for him.

In the championship fight with Douglas, Tyson was very slow and was settling for the power punches to win by a single punch. Douglas was more than ready for Tyson as he threw out the fight, from the beginning to the end of the fight, landed jabs, right crosses, and right uppercuts. Tyson wasn't able to avoid any of those punches. By the fifth round, Tyson's eyes were swollen. Tyson was able to land one power punch in the eighth round and knock Douglas down. Douglas got up to beat the count. After the eighth round, it was more of Douglas landing punches till he finally knocked Tyson out in the tenth round. This would be Tyson's first time being knocked down and knocked out.

Not only was Tyson not ready for Douglas in losing his title, but his cornermen was unprepared by not having ends well for Tyson's swollen eyes from the fifth round through the tenth round. They were using ice water in a latex glove. This didn't do Tyson any good; by the end of the fight, Tyson's eyes were swollen almost completely shut.

Like Jack Johnson and Muhammad Ali, Mike Tyson was added to the list of controversial fighters. Tyson began to get in trouble with the law and on the bad side of the public eye. His notorious actions consisted of public brawls, frolicking with women, charges of rape, and hasty marriages.

In 1992 Tyson was convicted of rape and denied bail. He was sentenced to six years in prison followed by four years of probation with mandatory psychiatric counseling.

Tyson would serve a portion of the six years and would continue his boxing career. He still had that top-contender edge and had a lot of love for the sport after so much time away from the sport.

After getting out of jail in 1995, he would have two fights in 1995, scoring two knockouts over Peter McNeeley and Buster Mathis Jr.

On September 7, 1996, he beat Bruce Seldon for the WBA title and then fought Holyfield. Tyson, starting in 1996, would be in two fights with Evander Holyfield. The first fight took place on November 9, 1996. Tyson would be a big favorite to win but lost the fight in eleven rounds by a TKO when the referee stopped the fight. After the fight, Tyson and his cornermen complained of Holyfield headbutting. Tyson lost his WBA title.

They would have a rematch on June 28, 1997. The rematch between Tyson and Holyfield is one of the most controversial fights in boxing history. In the fight Tyson got disqualified in three rounds for biting off part of Holyfield's ear. He had bitten both ears. The first time, he was warned by the referee. Tyson said he did it because of the headbutts from Holyfield.

The ear-biting incident was the most controversial event in all of sports. Tyson was fined three million dollars, and his boxing license was taken from him for one year.

After the ear-biting incident, Tyson's boxing career dried up. He received a chance to fight for the title for the last time in 2002 against the champion Lennox Lewis. At the age of thirty five, Tyson was knocked out in eight rounds in a one-sided fight by Lennox Lewis.

Tyson would lose three of his last four fights. The last fight he lost was to Kevin McBride, a journeyman fighter, by a TKO when he quit in the ring. This would be his last fight; he retired from the ring in 2005, saying he didn't have the heart anymore.

Tyson is considered one of the greatest punchers of all time. Out of the one hundred punchers of all time, he is rated sixteenth. After retiring from the ring, he fought in exhibitions to help support his bills.

Tyson filed for bankruptcy in 2003. It is believed that he made over three hundred million in his boxing career.

James "Buster" Douglas

Certainly one of the lowest points of Douglas's checkered professional career was this ninth-round kayo loss at the hands of journeyman Mike "the Giant" White in 1983.

An in-shape Douglas was in total control when he knocked out Tyson with this four-punch combination.

Douglas and his grandmother, Sarah Tones, admire his championship belt.

Mike "the Giant" White is motioned to a neutral corner by referee Larry Hazzard after knocking Douglas to the canvas during their fight in 1983 (above). White kayoed Douglas in the ninth round. A year later, however, Douglas stood toe-to-toe with Randall "Tax" Cobb to earn an upset majority decision (below). The victory placed him among the top twenty heavyweights in the world.

Bill Douglas got the heave-ho by the heavyweight champion after manager John Johnson issued him an ultimatum: "Either he goes, or I go."

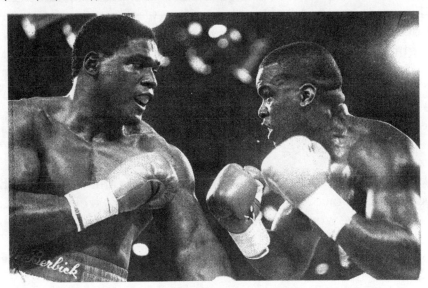

Douglas (right) seemed timid about putting a faded Trevor Berbick away, prompting cornerman Richie Giachetti to scream, "He has no heart."

233

James "Buster" Douglas

Born: 1960, Ohio
Weight: 230 lbs., 6'4"
Champion: 1990-1991

Won: 38   Lost: 6   Drew: 1   Knockout: 25

Buster Douglas was a gifted boxer with exceptional speed, good jab, and coordination. He also was an up-and-down unheard-of fighter who had his one big opportunity and who took great advantage of it.

Growing up, Douglas was an athlete playing football and basketball in high school. He is the son of a professional fighter, William "Dynamite" Douglas, who was a contender as a middleweight and as a light heavyweight. It was his father who taught his son Buster to box at the Blackburn recreation center.

Douglas had his first professional fight on May 31, 1981, when he won by a TKO over Dan O'Malley. After the O'Malley fight, he would win a total of five fights in a row. On his sixth fight, he would lose his first fight; this fight would be against David Bey on November 6, 1981, by a knockout. For the Bey fight, he was overweight.

Douglas did not follow the usual path to the championship because of his inconsistent performances and his weight problem. Sometimes he would come in the ring in great shape, and other times he would come in the ring twenty pounds overweight. You never knew which Douglas you would get. His weigh was constantly up and down.

After being knocked out by Bey, he would go on to win another six fights in a row, then have a draw with Steffen Tangstad on October 16, 1982. After the draw with Tangstad, once again he would go on a winning streak, this time winning seven fights in a row. On his eighth fight, he fought Mike White on December 17,

1983. For the White fight, he came in the ring overweight but was still leading big on rounds. Leading big on rounds did not help him because he got tired and knocked out in the ninth round.

When Douglas fought Randall "Tex" Cobb on November 9, 1984, he won by a decision and cracked the top twenty in ranking. Then he came into the ring overweight at 242 pounds against Jesse Ferguson on May 9, 1985, losing to Ferguson by a decision. Fight fans still didn't know what to expect from Douglas with his winning streak and then to lose a fight to a fighter who was not to a top contender to the title.

Douglas started to make a name for himself when he trimmed down to 230 pounds to fight a top-ten fighter in Greg Page who he beat by a decision; now boxing fans began to look at him as a good fighter and a top contender.

This win over Page set him up to fight Tony Tucker for the vacant IBF championship on May 30, 1987. This would be Douglas's first fight for any kind of championship. He lost to Tucker by a knockout in the tenth round.

After the loss to Tucker, Douglas would win another six fights in a row from 1988 to 1990. His last two fights were wins over top contenders in Trevor Berbick and Oliver McCall. He won by a unanimous ten-round decision over both of them. These two wins over Berbick and McCall set him up for a title shot with the undisputed champion Mike Tyson.

Mike Tyson signed to defend his title against Buster Douglas on February 11, 1990. Going into the fight with Tyson, nobody gave Douglas a chance of winning. After thirty-five fights, some people thought that he lacked courage; some thought he was overrated; some even thought that he should find another line of work because of his past record of inconsistency. Douglas was a big 42-1 underdog, and everybody figured it was another quick knockout for Tyson, who most people thought was invincible in the ring. Even Tyson said that he was "the baddest man on the planet."

Douglas would have some advantages in this fight that a lot of boxing fans did not know. First of all, he had trained very hard, was in good shape, and took Tyson seriously as a fighter. Tyson didn't take Douglas seriously. Most of the fighters who fought Tyson were intimidated by Tyson before the bell rang.

For this fight, Douglas was not going to be intimidated. Douglas was so much bigger than Tyson in arm reach by twelve inches; he knew he could hit Tyson with jabs and fighting from a distance.

Douglas's mother, Lula Pearl, would die twenty three days before the fight. Her son had already convinced her that he was going to win before she died. Some people wonder if Douglas would or could fight after his mother's death. He would say that he would fight and that it would intensify him.

In the title fight, Douglas fought the fight of his life, never looking better. Douglas fought a smart fight. He used his big-reach advantage in landing long left jabs and hard right hand to the head to control the fight from the beginning to the end of the fight. For ten rounds Tyson couldn't get past Douglas's jabs and lead right crosses. Except for Tyson landing a power right to Douglas's head in the eighth round for a knockout, Douglas's jabs and reach kept him from Tyson's power punches.

After ten rounds of almost hitting Tyson at will, he knocked Tyson out in the tenth round to win the title. With Douglas winning, it was the biggest upset in heavyweight history. He was now the undisputed champion of the world.

After the Tyson fight, Douglas went down as a fighter, and he had health problems. In Douglas's first defense of his title, he signs to fight Evander Holyfield on October 26, 1990. For this title fight, Douglas came into the ring overweight by almost twenty pounds and looked it. Being out of shape, the fight lasted just three rounds with Holyfield winning by a knockout and becoming the new champion.

After losing his title to Holyfield, fight fans thought that it was one of the most disgraceful performances in the heavyweight history.

For the Holyfield fight, Douglas got 24.6 million; after the fight he would retire, lie back, gain weight, and get sick. His weight would go over four hundred pounds; he was sluggish, and his sugar level was high. His life at this time was out of control since the Holyfield fight.

Douglas's health would get better, and he got his weight down and made a comeback to the ring in 1996. He would have his first fight in six years on June 22, 1996, against Tony LaRosa;

he would win by a TKO in four rounds. Douglas would win six fights in a row. On his seventh fight, he would be fighting Lou Savare in 1998. Savare knocked out Douglas in the first round.

After the Savare fight, Douglas would have two more fights, both wins for him. The last fight was against Andre Crowder, which he won on February 19, 1999.

Douglas is now involved in real estate, building condominiums, and retail development in the Douglas Development and Community Building.

Evander Holyfield

Power: When Holyfield kayoed Buster Douglas with one punch, he silenced some of the critics who had questioned his finishing touch.

Battle of the ages: In his first title defense, Holyfield pummeled forty-two-year-old former champion George Foreman en route to a twelve-round unanimous decision in Atlantic City.

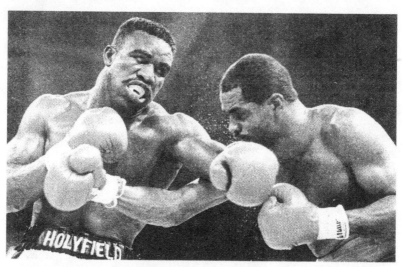

An eighth-round knockout of Carlos DeLeon unified the cruiserweight title and set the stage for Holyfield's invasion of the heavyweight ranks. A lot of skeptics said he was too small to become heavyweight champion, and when he proved them wrong, few were candid enough to admit their error.

Evander Holyfield

Born: 1962, Alabama
Weight: 205 lbs., 6'2"
Champion: 1990-1992

Won: 42   Lost: 10   Drew: 2   Knockouts: 27

One of the few heavyweight champions to win a title in two weight divisions. Evander Holyfield was a very dedicated fighter in the gym when preparing for a fight, always in tip-top shape. He always fought in a relentless, aggressive way and had great recuperative ability.

Holyfield began boxing at the age of twelve when he won the Boys Club boxing tournament. Living in Georgia, he won the South Eastern Regional Champion at fifteen years of age. Fighting as an amateur, Holyfield would win the Golden Gloves in 1984.

In 1984 Holyfield would be invited to the 1984 Olympics. In the finals Holyfield was involved in a controversial disqualification for kayoing his opponent after the referee had called break; this caused him to miss a chance to win a gold medal, instead winning the bronze.

After the Olympics, Holyfield turned pro in 1984 fighting as a light heavyweight. He would have his first fight on November 15, 1984, against Lionel Byarm whom he beat in six rounds. Holyfield would go on and win his first four fights in 1984, all as a light heavyweight fighter in all.

In 1985, Holyfield would move up in weight and fight as a cruiserweight. He had his first fight as a cruiserweight fighter on July 20, 1985, against Tyrone Booze whom he would beat by a decision. Holyfield would go on and win seven straight fights as a cruiserweight, six of them by knockout. He became the number one contender to fight the champion Dwight Muhammad Qawi.

Holyfield and Qawi fought for the WBA title on July 12, 1986. In the fight Holyfield won a tough fifteen-round split decision over Qawi, but Qawi wasn't the only cruiserweight champion, just the WBA champion. In May of 1987, Holyfield beat Ricky Parkey in three rounds to be recognized as the IBF champion. Then in April of 1988, he defeated Carlos de Leon; Holyfield was now the undisputed cruiserweight champion of the world.

Holyfield would defend his title six times from 1986 to 1988, winning all by knockout. One of the six was a rematch with the former champion Dwight Muhammad Qawi; this time he knocked out Qawi in four rounds.

By the middle of 1988, Holyfield had beaten all the top contenders in the cruiserweight division. He began to think of the heavyweight division and fighting Mike Tyson for the heavyweight title. He gave up his cruiserweight title and started fighting as a heavyweight toward the end of 1988.

On July 16, 1988, Holyfield had his first fight as a heavyweight against James "Quick" Tillis, whom he would beat by a fifth-round knockout. A lot of people thought he wasn't a true heavyweight because he started his professional career as a light heavyweight and later a cruiserweight.

He would prove all of them wrong by beating the heavyweight top contender. Holyfield would win six straight fights as a heavyweight from 1988 to 1990. In those six wins, he had wins over top contenders Pinklon Thomas, Michael Dokes, and Alex Stewart, working his way up to the number one contender to the title.

Holyfield would stay the number one contender longer than he should have to get a shot at the title. Longer than any other top contender in the last ten years, he never got the shot at Tyson's title. Tyson would fight Buster Douglas in 1990, even though Douglas was ranked higher than Holyfield.

With Tyson losing his title to Douglas, Holyfield's eyes were now on Douglas for the title. Finally on October 25, 1990, Holyfield got his chance to fight Buster Douglas for the title. For the fight Holyfield was in great shape at 208 lbs., and Douglas was way out of shape at 246. It wasn't much of a fight for Holyfield; he fought a good fight, won the first two rounds, and knocked Douglas out in the third round from a hard right to become the new heavyweight champion of the world and the undisputed champion.

For the next two years, Holyfield would be champion; he was criticized about who he fought and how he won. In his first defense of his title, he fought the former heavyweight champion George Foreman who was forty-two years old on the fight on April 19, 1991. Holyfield won by unanimous decision but failed to really hurt the old Foreman, failed to stop him, and Foreman staggered him.

On Holyfield's second defense of his title, he fought a journey fighter named Bert Cooper on November 23, 1991. This would be a tough fight for Holyfield; he would have to survive the first knockdown of his professional career in the third round. Holyfield would go on and punish Cooper in the seventh round and win by a TKO in seven rounds.

On his third defense of his title, he fought Larry Holmes who also was forty-two years old on June 19, 1992. Holyfield would win by a unanimous decision, but he did not really hurt Holmes.

With these three defenses of his title against two old fighters of forty-two and against a journey fighter that knocked him down, boxing fans were having doubts about Holyfield. They wondered why he couldn't knock out two former champions who were forty-two years old and then getting knocked down by Cooper, who took the fight on with only six days' notice as a fill-in.

On the fourth defense of his title, Holyfield fought top contender Riddick Bowe on November 13, 1992. This would be his toughest challenger. In this fight Holyfield weighed in at 205 lbs., to Bowe's 235 pounds. Bowe was much bigger and stronger, but for most of the fight, Holyfield went toe-to-toe with Bowe. Holyfield showed courage in going toe-to-toe with a fighter outweighing him by thirty pounds. He was knocked down in the eleventh round and was taking a beating. He lost his title to Bowe by a unanimous decision. This would be Holyfield's first loss in twenty-nine fights.

After losing his title to Bowe, Holyfield wanted to get his title back. Starting out he would beat Alex Stewart by a decision on June 26, 1993. Then came the rematch with Riddick Bowe. They fought on November 6, 1993, in a strange fight where the fight was held up for twenty minutes because of a man parachuting from the ceiling. After everything was restored to order, Holyfield would go on and win his title back by a split decision.

After winning his title back from Bowe, Holyfield had his first defense of his title on April 22, 1994, against Michael Moorer. In the fight against Moorer, Holyfield would land a hard left that floored Moorer in round two. Moorer's jab would be working excellent in this fight and would win by a decision over Holyfield to win the title.

After losing his title to Moorer, Holyfield was diagnosed with a heart condition in 1994 and retired from the ring. By 1995 he had passed his examination by the boxing commission. Getting back in the ring, he would beat a top contender, Ray Mercer, on May 20, 1995. Then came the third fight with Riddick Bowe on November 4, 1995. In the Bowe fight, Holyfield would knock Bowe down in the fight, but Bowe would knock Holyfield out in eight rounds.

Holyfield would have two fights with Mike Tyson. The first one on November 9, 1996, he beat Tyson by a TKO in eleven rounds and won the WBA title. In the second fight on June 26, 1997, Holyfield would beat Tyson by a disqualification in the third round after he had bit part of Holyfield's upper ear off and spit it out on the ring floor.

In a rematch with Michael Moorer on November 8, 1997, Holyfield this time would avenge for the loss he had the first time by winning on a TKO over Moorer. In the fight he knocks Moorer down, and the referee stopped the fight, and Holyfield won the IBF title.

The fight everybody wanted to see was the unification of belts between Holyfield and Lennox Lewis. These were the two fighters with all the belts. Holyfield had the IBA and the WBA version, and Lew had the other three belts.

Holyfield and Lewis fought to undivide the championship on March 13, 1999. The fight ended in a draw that many people thought Lewis had won easily. They would have a rematch on November 11, 1999. In their rematch Lewis won by unanimous decision to be the undisputed heavyweight champion of the world.

After the loss to Lewis, Holyfield would win more fights, lose more fights, fight for more titles, and win the WBA title from John Ruiz in 2000; but none would be for the undisputed title like the Lewis fight.

Holyfield would lose three straight fights from the end of 2002 to 2004. He lost to Chris Byrd in 2002, in 2003 to James Toney by a TKO, and in 2004 to Larry Donald. At the age of forty-two, people wanted him to retire from the ring, but Holyfield would continue.

Holyfield didn't fight at all in 2005. From 2006 through 2008, Holyfield had six fights winning four and losing two. He fought Nikalov Valuev on December 20, 2008, believed to be his last fight at the age of forty-six. In the Valuev fight, he lost by a decision to Valuev.

In Holyfield's boxing career, he did a lot of boxing. When he was fighting as a cruiserweight and as the cruiserweight champion, he dominated it. He was very responsible for the recognition that the division got; at that time the cruiserweight was kind of new. Fighting as a heavyweight, he proved people wrong who believed he was an overblown light heavyweight.

Holyfield is a fighter that will be remembered as a fighter with the finest qualities, tremendous pride, a heart, and an overwhelming desire to win. He also made money by appearing on television, in movies, and product endorsements while he was still fighting.

Riddick Bowe

Bowe couldn't knock out Evander Holyfield.

Bert Cooper couldn't hurt Bowe.

Donald's fast hands tortured Mike Dixon.

Rock's smiling now, but if he only knew what 1994 has in store for Team Bowe.

Bowe's comeback was almost derailed in his second bout when journeyman Billy Zumbrun gave him all he could handle. While Bowe squeaked by on a controversial and unpopular decision, the former heavyweight champion took a lot of punishment, which raised additional concerns about his health.

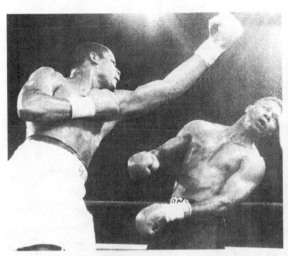

Warming up for 1994? Rock and Riddick are quite a team.

Biggs often found himself on the receiving end of Bowe's lethal bombs. After eight sizzling rounds in this matchup of former Olympic medalists, Bowe chalked one up for the class of '88.

Martin landed several hard lefts before sustaining a cut that ended the bout. The premature stoppage saved Bowe further embarrassment.

Bowe was a lean, mean fighting machine when he starched contender Bruce Seldon last year. He hasn't shown the same tenacity since.

245

Riddick Bowe

Born: 1967, New York
Weight: 230 lbs., 6'5"
Champion: 1992-1993

Won: 43   Lost: 1   Drew: 0   Knockouts: 33

Riddick Bowe was a very big fighter, strong with hitting power. Some fight fans question his heart and dedication.

Fighting as an amateur, Bowe was a successful fighter. He won the New York Golden Gloves four times, winning the Golden Gloves in 1985 and 1986 at 178 pounds, and 1987 and 1988 as a super heavyweight. In the 1988 Seoul Olympic, he won a silver medal, losing the gold medal to Lennox Lewis by a two-round knockout.

Going into the 1998 Olympics, Bowe was a favorite to win the gold. When he lost to Lennox Lewis by a two-round knockout, people thought it was a disappointing performance. His critics said that he lacked the heart and desire to become a champion.

After his performance in the 1988 Olympics, some managers and promoters turned their backs on Bowe. One of the few fight people who had confidence in Bowe was Rock Newman, who became his manager in December of 1988. Newman's plan was to move Bowe from the drug in housing development in Brooklyn, New York, to live in Maryland. Newman's next move was to get the legendary Eddie Futch to train him.

Bowe had his first professional fight in March of 1989 against Lionel Butler, whom he knocked out in two rounds. The year 1989 would be a busy year for Bowe, having thirteen professional fights, although not against good fighters.

In 1990 Bowe would have two wins over good fighters in Pinklon Thomas whom he stopped in eighth round, and a two-round knockout over Bert Cooper. With the two wins, he now was a ranked opponent

In 1991 and 1992, Bowe beat all the top contenders. In March of 1991, he knocked out the Olympic gold medalist Tyrell Biggs, then he beat by decision Tony Tucker; in August of 1991 he knocked out Pierre Coetzer. By now Bowe was the number one contender to fight the champion Evander Holyfield.

In November of 1992, Evander Holyfield and Riddick Bowe fought for the heavyweight championship of the world. This would be a very tough fight for both fighters. In the fight Bowe would land a lot of punishing blows to Holyfield throughout the fight. Holyfield fought well, a very game fighter, and he continued to fight but paying a price. In the eleventh round, Bowe landed two rights that spun Holyfield into the ropes. Bowe than landed another right that knocked Holyfield to his knees. Holyfield got up and continued to fight. Bowe would win the fight on a unanimous decision. Bowe would say later, "I hit Evander with everything. He has the heart of a lion." By winning the fight against Holyfield, Bowe became the undisputed heavyweight champion of the world.

Bowe, now the champion, had two successful defenses of his title in 1993. He first fought Michael Dokes in February, where he would knock Dokes out in one round. His second defense of the title was against Jesse Ferguson in May, where he would knock Ferguson out in two rounds.

Before these two fights with Dokes and Ferguson, Bowe lost a lot of image as champion when he refused to fight the WBC number one contender Lennox Lewis, the same Lennox Lewis who had knocked him out in two rounds at the 1988 Olympics; instead of fighting Lewis, he dumped the WBC belt in the trash can.

In Bowe's third defense of his title, he fought a rematch with Evander Holyfield on November 6, 1993; in the one year that Bowe was champion, his weight had bloomed from the 235 pounds he weigh when he won the title to as high as 288 pounds. For his rematch with Holyfield, he weighed 246 pounds, which was too much for him; and he was not in good shape. It still was a great fight with both fighters landing power punches. Bowe lost the fight and his title by a decision.

After the loss of his title to Holyfield, Bowe had four straight victories then had a third fight with Evander Holyfield on November 14, 1995. In the fight, it was war again between the two fighters. Holyfield knocked Bowe down in the sixth round from a left hook. Bowe would get up and knock Holyfield out in the eighth round.

In 1996 Bowe would have two fights with Andrew Golota where he was trailing on the scorecard in both fights but would win both on disqualifications. The first fight on July 11, Golota, leading on points, was also repeatedly hitting Bowe in the testicles and got disqualified in seven rounds. In their rematch Golota, again leading on points into the ninth round, hit Bowe with three straight hard blows to the testicles, to be disqualified yet again. Before that he was giving Bowe a sound beating with two knockdowns.

After the Golota fight, Bowe retired from the ring. When he retired from boxing, it was clear to everyone, with the two fights with Andrew Golota, that Bowe had gone down a lot as a fighter and that he had a weight problem even though he was only twenty-nine years old.

Being retired from the ring was not good to Bowe. He couldn't keep a job, he stayed in trouble, and he did time. He joined the United States Marine Corps where he stayed a little over a week and saw it wasn't for him and was able to get out of it. From the marine corps, Bowe got in trouble with the law from battering assault to kidnapping. For the kidnapping of his wife and kids, he would serve eighteen months in jail.

After being out of the ring for seven years, Bowe made a comeback to the ring on September 25, 2004 with a second-round knockout of Marcus Rhode. He weighed 263 pounds for the fight. Had another comeback fight in April of 2005 against Billy Zumbrun, a journeyman that he barely beat and who weighed 280 lbs. for the fight.

In 2005 Bowe would claim bankruptcy. On December 13, 2008, Bowe would make yet another comeback after three and a half years from the ring, at the age of forty-one. He fought Gene Pukall, whom he beat in eight rounds.

After having made seventy-five million in boxing, today Bowe has little of his money. He still wants to fight in 2009 to make money if the purse is good.

Bowe would be looked at as a good fighter, with a good jab and a big fighter. He will also be looked at as a fighter who could have been better if he trained properly and stayed in shape. From the second Holyfield fight until the end of his career, he was always overweight.

Michael Moorer

Michael Moorer

Moorer deserved the decision . . . but just barely.

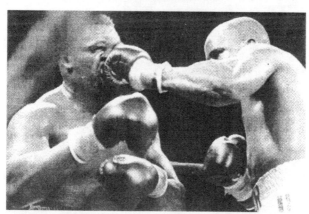

Moorer is about to finish Cooper with a left in round five. A head-snapping right uppercut would soon follow. The combination punctuated Moorer's gritty performance.

Expect Moorer to do more of this.

It looks like people's champion George Foreman will fight Michael Moorer again in early 1996. But even if he wins, it could very well be Foreman's last fight. Then again, you never know with Big George.

By round five, Moorer was in control of the fight. Cooper, who had a cut above his right eye, was beginning to tire; and a potent two-punch combination knocked him down and out.

Michael Moorer

Born: 1967
Weight: 230 lbs., 6'2"
Champion: 1994-1994

Won: 52   Lost: 4   Drew: 1   Knockouts: 40

Michael Moorer as a fighter was a good boxer and puncher with power. He had maybe the best start of a professional boxing career than any fighter in any division. In his first year as a professional, he would win twelve straight fights and be champion in his first year as a fighter. Moorer would also win his first twenty-six fights by knockout.

As an amateur fighter, Moorer had a record of 48-16. At the Goodwill Game, he won a bronze medal as a light middleweight. In 1986 he won the United States Amateur Light Middleweight championship at 156 pounds.

Moorer had his first professional fight on March 4, 1988, scoring a first-round knockout of Adrian Riggs. Starting his career, Moorer was fighting as a light heavyweight.

Fighting as a light heavyweight, Moorer would win his first twelve fights all by knockouts. His twelfth fight would be a fifth-round TKO over Ramzi Hassan for the vacant WBO light heavyweight title.

As the light heavyweight champion, Moorer would defend his title nine times from 1989 through 1990. For two years fighting as a light heavyweight, he was unbeatable, terrorizing the division, and was 22-0 all by knockouts.

While Moorer held the WBO light heavyweight title, there were other light heavyweight champions. Virgil Hill held the WBA title, and Prince Charles held the IBF title. Moore wanted to unify the belts but never got the chance.

So Moorer never got the big-money fights as a light heavyweight. He was also having a weight problem making the 175 pound weight limit. Within nine years he was fighting at 230 pounds. Moorer had his last fight as a light heavyweight in December 1990 when he knocked out Danny Lindstrom. He skipped over the cruiserweight division, a division that he probably could have dominated like he did the light heavyweight division.

In 1991, Moorer gave up the light heavyweight title to fight as a heavyweight. Fighting as a heavyweight in 1991, he had four fights, winning all of them by knockouts. By May 15, 1992, Moorer had won six straight heavyweight fights by knockouts when he fought Bert Cooper for the WBO title. In the Bert Cooper fight, Moorer proved that he could fight heavyweight and could take heavyweight punches and a beating.

The Moorer and Cooper fight happened on May 15, 1992. In the fight Cooper knocked Moorer down in the first forty seconds of the first round by backing Moorer into a corner, hitting him with both hands until Moorer fell to the floor. Moorer showed recuperation spirit by getting up and later landed two rights that floored Cooper; in the third round, Cooper landed a hard right that hurt Moorer, then landed lefts and rights to knock Moorer down for the second time in the fight. In the fifth and final round, Moorer landed a hard right uppercut and a straight left and knocked him down. Cooper got up, and the referee stopped it. Moorer would say later that Cooper did hurt him a couple of times in the fight.

Winning the WBO title didn't really mean too much to Moorer by him never defending it. He would win five straight fights with a victory over contender James "Bone Crusher" Smith. These wins got him the chance he wanted to fight the real champion Evander Holyfield.

On April 22, 1994, Moorer got to fight the real champion Evander Holyfield. Moorer came into the fight as 12-0 as a heavyweight fighter, a professional record of 34-0, and a 2-1 underdog to lose.

In the fight, Moorer fought the fight of his career, taking every bit of punishment Holyfield could administer. In the first round, he was jabbing excellently; and in the second round, he was making headway and still jabbing excellently and appeared to have Holyfield in trouble. Suddenly with only twenty-five seconds left in the round, Moorer was moving in confidently when he was caught flush by a thunderous left. Moorer went down and was up before the mandatory eight-second count. Moorer would go on and outbox Holyfield to win by a decision to be the new world heavyweight champion.

In winning the title from Evander Holyfield, he became the first left-handed (southpaw) heavyweight champion ever. Only two left-handers had fought for the heavyweight title, Karl Mildenberger and Richard Dunn. Muhammad Ali defeated both of them.

Being the champion now, Moorer made his first title defense on November 5, 1994, against the former world champion George Foreman. In the fight, Moorer was pretty much hitting Foreman at will, moving away, with Foreman coming forward. Moorer was winning all the rounds and leading on all three scorecards. In the tenth round, Foreman landed a hard right to Moorer's chin, and he went down and was counted out. In losing, Moorer lost his title and lost his first professional fight, now 35-1.

After losing his title to Foreman, Moorer would still have success. He would win four straight fights, including inning the IBF title from Axel Schulz by a decision on June 22, 1996.

Then there came the rematch with Evander Holyfield on November 8, 1997. In this match, Moorer would be knocked down a total of five times before the fight was stopped in the eighth round. After the loss, he would retire from the ring.

After being retired from the ring for three years, he would make a comeback. His comeback to the ring would happen on November 17, 2000, when he fought Lorenzo Boyd, whom he would knock out in four rounds. He would have success in his comeback from 2000 to 2002 by being undefeated in five straight fights. Then on August 17, 2002, Moorer would suffer a thirty-second, first-round loss to David Tua.

Even with the bad loss to David Tua, Moorer continued to fight. Moorer would win his next three fights. On his fourth fight on July 3, 2004, he would lose to Elico Castillo by a unanimous decision. After the loss to Castillo, Moorer would fight five more times, winning all of them. His last of those fights would be his last professional fight, February 8, 2008, against Shelby Gross, whom he knocked out.

With his boxing career now over, Moorer has worked as a boxing trainer and has worked as guest, commentating on fight cards.

Lennox Lewis

Lennox Lewis helped change the perception of English heavyweights by going undefeated in the U.S. His eighth-round knockout of Mike Tyson in 2002 cemented his legacy as one of, if not the best, British fighter of all-time. All told, Lewis won 22 fights in the United States.

Lennox Lewis

Evander Holyfield was viewed by many as the best heavyweight of this era until Lewis defeated him in 1999. Though Holyfield was past his prime at the time, the results of their two fights have helped sway that debate in Lewis's direction.

Trainer Emanuel Steward has insisted for years that Lewis is the best big man since Muhammad Ali. Based on Lewis's last two performances, Steward may have a valid argument.

Lewis sent Williams for a pony ride.

Lewis served as a color commentator alongside Col. Bob Sheridan for the international broadcast of the Chris Byrd–Evander Holyfield fight in December. Over Lewis's right shoulder, you can see promoter Don King, who seems to be wielding ever-increasing influence over the champ.

Lennox Lewis

Born: 1965, England
Weight: 240 lbs., 6'5"
Champion: 1999-2001, 2001-2004

Won: 41   Lost: 2   Drew: 1   Knockouts: 32

Lennox Lewis was a very big fighter who could box well and could slug and hit with power—a champion who fought anyone and beat everybody that he fought, including the two losses he had. The problem was the champions Mike Tyson and Riddick Bowe wouldn't fight him in the nineties.

Lewis was born in England; he would move to Canada by 1977. In high school he was a gifted athlete in football, soccer, and basketball. He would later like boxing as his favorite sport.

Starting out as an amateur in 1983, Lewis was seventeen years old. He would win a lot, starting with World Amateur junior title in 1983. Fighting as a Canadian, he was a dominant Canadian fighter by the time he was eighteen years old. In the 1984 Los Angeles Olympics, he represented Canada as a super heavyweight. He made it all the way to the quarter finals where he lost by a decision to American Tyrell Biggs, who would go on and win the gold medal.

Lewis knew that by him advancing as far as he did in the 1984 Olympics, he could have turned pro right then and made big money. But Lewis had a goal, and his goal was to go on to the 1988 Olympics and win the gold medal. For this, he would stay an amateur fighter for four more years and win a lot more medals.

In the next four years, Lewis would win medals in everything he tried. In 1985 he won a silver medal in the World Cup competition. In 1986 he won a gold medal in the Commonwealth Game as a super heavyweight. In 1987 he won a silver medal

258

at the Pan American Games as a super heavyweight. In 1987 Lewis would also win the North American super heavyweight championship. In 1988 came what Lewis had worked so hard and long for, the 1988 Seoul Olympics. This time he would not lose. Lewis beat United States' Riddick Bowe by a two-round TKO in the final to win the gold medal for Canada. He had an amateur record of 75-7.

After winning his gold medal, Lewis turned pro and moved back to England. He had his first professional fight on June 27, 1989, fighting Al Malcolm whom he would knock out in two rounds. Starting out, Lewis won a lot of his fights by knockouts, but not by fighting good fighters and fighting mostly in England.

Lewis twelfth fight would be against a fighter who had a name in the ring in Ossie Ocasio, who had fought Larry Holmes for the heavyweight title in 1979. Lewis fought Ossie Ocasio on June 27, 1990, winning by a decision over Ocasio. Lewis now fought better fighters, and now he had a record of 12-0.

By 1990, Lewis was thinking of the overseas belts, where he was doing most of his fights. On October 31, 1990, he fought Jean Chanet for the European heavyweight title. He beat Chanet by a knockout in six rounds to be the European champion. Having won the European title, Lewis now set his eyes on the British title. On March 6, 1991, he fought Gary Mason for the British title. Lewis beat Mason by a seventh-round knockout to be the British and European heavyweight champion.

Lewis came to the United States for two fights in 1991 to make his name even bigger as a fighter. First he fought Mike Weaver on July 12, 1991. Like Ossie Ocasio, he had fought Larry Holmes for the title in 1979. In this fight Lewis knocked Weaver out in six rounds. Then came the fight with Tyrell Biggs on November 23, 1991; in this fight Lewis would get the chance to get revenge on Tyrell Biggs who had beaten him for the gold medal in the 1984 Olympics. This time Lewis would not lose in knocking Biggs out in three rounds.

With Lewis already having the British and European belts, there was still one more belt overseas that he wanted. The next belt he wanted was the Commonwealth Heavyweight title. The fight for this title was against Derek Williams on April 30, 1992. In this fight, Lewis knocked Williams out in three rounds to now have all three belts: the British, the European, and now the Commonwealth championship. Now having all three of these belts and having beaten Tyrell Biggs, a contender to the title, Lewis was now a top-five contender to the world heavyweight title in 1992.

Lewis now wanted the world title. To get closer to the world championship, he fought the number one contender to the title Donovan "Razor" Ruddock on October 31, 1992. Lewis knocked out Ruddock in two rounds to become the new number one contender to the world title with a record of 22-0.

Now being the number one contender after beating Ruddock, Lewis had a problem. The problem was that the undisputed world heavyweight championship Riddick Bowe refused to fight him. By Bowe refusing to fight him, Bowe was willing to lose the WBC version of the heavyweight title. The WBC version of the title was given to Lewis in January of 1993. Bowe still had all of the other belts, including the Lineal belt, which says to be the true champion, you have to beat the true champion. Bowe was still looked at by mostly everyone as the true champion.

With the WBC belt now, Lewis had three straight wins defending the title, beating Tony Tucker, Frank Bruno, and Phil Jackson. On Lewis's fourth defense of the title on September 24, 1994, he fought Oliver McCall. In this fight McCall landed a hard right to the chin and knocked Lewis down. Lewis would get up in time, but the referee thought that he couldn't continue and stopped the fight. Lewis lost by a TKO in two rounds, lost his WBC title, and had his first professional loss; now he was 25-1.

From January of 1993 to September of 1994, when Lewis won and lost the WBC title, it is believed by most, including myself, that Riddick Bowe, Evander Holyfield, and Michael Moore were the real champions during this time. They were the champions who beat the champion in the ring.

Mike Tyson in 1996 had the WBC version of the title, and other fighters had the other belts to the championship. It was in 1995 and will continue to be until 1999. Lewis had won four straight fights after he lost to McCall. Two of his wins were over top contender Ray Mercer and Tommy Morrison. He was the number one contender, and he wanted to fight Mike Tyson for the WBC title. Tyson was told by the WBC to fight Lewis or give up the WBC title. Tyson did not want to fight Lewis, so he gave up the WBC title. He fought Evander Holyfield instead.

This set up a rematch with Oliver McCall to fight for the new vacant WBC title. Lewis and McCall fought the rematch for the WBC title on February 7, 1997. This would be one of the strangest fights in heavyweight history. After the third round, McCall refused to fight in round four and round five and was crying in the ring. The referee had to stop the fight and gave the win to Lewis on a TKO.

Like Mike Tyson in the late '80s, Lewis had to win each belt separately to be recognized as the undisputed champion of the world. With the WBC title, he defended it four times with wins over Andrew Golota in one round and Shannon Briggs in five rounds. Then there was the fight to unify the belts with Evander Holyfield on March 13, 1999. The fight would end in controversy as Lewis with over twice as many punches as Holyfield (348-130), at times hitting Holyfield at will. At the end of the fight it was scored a draw.

A rematch was ordered right away with Lewis and Holyfield. The rematch was on November 13, 1999. This fight was for all the marbles. The two of them had all the belts, the WBC, IBF, WBA, and the IBO title. This time Lewis won by a unanimous decision and became the undisputed heavyweight champion of the world. Now with all the belts, for this reason I start his reign as world champion with this unification fight with Holyfield.

After the win over Holyfield, Lewis had three defenses of his title, winning all of them. On his fourth defense, he fought Hasim Rahman on April 22, 2001. Lewis was a big favorite to win in this fight but got knocked out by Rahman in the fifth round. Lewis would get a rematch with Rahman on November 17, 2001. This time in the rematch, Lewis took care of business by knocking out Rahman in the fourth round.

Next up for Lewis was a fight with Mike Tyson on June 8, 2002. This was a fight that everybody wanted to see and figured to be a great fight. It was anything but a great fight. It was an easy one-sided fight for Lewis as he dominated every round and knocked Tyson out in the eighth round.

For Lewis's next fight, he fought the number one contender Vitali Klitschko on June 21, 2003. The fight with Klitschko was a very tough fight for Lewis as Klitschko won the early rounds. Lewis fought better in the middle rounds and opened a cut above Klitschko's left eye in the third round. Before the start of the seventh round, the doctor looked at Klitschko's badly cut eye and decided that the fight should be stopped. Lewis won by a TKO in seven rounds. When the fight was stopped, Klitschko was leading on all three scorecards.

The Lewis and Klitschko fight was such a good and even fight that everybody wanted a rematch. But there would be no rematch; the fight with Klitschko was to be his last fight; he retired from the ring.

Retired now, Lewis has done film and some boxing commentating for HBO. He has been elected to both the Canada Sports Hall of Fame and the International Boxing Hall of Fame.

Hasim Rahman

Rahman plows a right into the head of Tua.

Can lightning strike a third time? Lewis's shock knockout losses to Oliver McCall and Hasim Rahman (pictured) both damaged his reputation, and there's no telling how much another kayo loss would affect his standing among the all-time greats.

Hasim Rahman

Born: 1972, Maryland
Weight: 235 lbs., 6'2"
Champion: 2001-2001

Won: 45   Lost: 7   Drew: 2   Knockouts: 36

Rahman was a very hard-hitting champion who was versatile, had a consistent jab and heart. He, unlike most fighters, started his boxing career at a late age. Growing up in a tough neighborhood in Baltimore, Rahman had a rough early life. He was a tough guy, had lots of street fights, was an enforcer for drug dealers, and got himself shot five times. He knew that if he didn't straighten up soon, he would either be in a penitentiary or dead from being in trouble with the law so much.

Rahman went to the Mac Lewis gym to keep out of trouble. He was discovered by a neighborhood former professional boxer. He started his amateur career at the age of twenty and had only ten fights.

Rahman had his first professional fight on December 3, 1994, against Gregory Herrington, whom he knocked out in one round. In 1995 he would have nine fights, winning all of them. In 1996 Rahman would top that off with eleven fights, winning all of them also. His biggest fight in 1996 was on October 15, 1996, against Trevor Berbick, a top contender. Rahman won by unanimous decision over Berbick.

1997 would be a good year for Rahman. He would have four fights and would win all of them. He would also have two titles. The first was won on July 15, 1997, when he fought and beat Jeff Wooden for the vacant USBA heavyweight title. On November 1, 1997, he fought and beat Obed Sullivan to win the IBF Intercontinental heavyweight title.

With a record of 20-0 winning mostly by knockouts, the boxing world could see that he had power in his punches. Rahman fought David Tua on December 29, 1998. Tua, like Rahman, was also a top contender. In the fight, Rahman was winning almost every round. At the end of the ninth round after the bell, Tua hit Rahman with a punch that dazed him. Not given extra minutes to recover from the late punch, he was right back out for the tenth round. In the tenth round, Tua was all over him, landing punches, until the referee stopped it. This would be Rahman's first professional loss.

After the David Tua loss, Rahman would win two fights by knockouts in 1999. In his third fight on November 6, 1999, he would have his second loss as a professional. It was by an eighth-round knockout from Oleg Maskaer. Rahman thought this was an easy fight and didn't train hard for it. This loss to Maskaer would also take him out of the top ten as a contender.

Rahman won three straight fights in 2000 to get his ranking back. One of his wins was over Corrie Sanders, a ranked contender to the title, on March 20, 2000. Sanders had Rahman down twice in the fight, but Rahman knocked him out in the seventh round. He was now a contender to the title with these three wins. He had earned a title match with Lennox Lewis on April 21, 2001.

Rahman was a big 20-1 underdog going into the Lewis fight. Both fighters landed hard punches through the five rounds, but Rahman was behind in points. Rahman suffered a cut above the eye in the fifth round but continued to throw hard punches. Lewis was still throwing hard hooks, uppercuts, and crosses in the fifth round. Rahman caught Lewis with a hard right cross to Lewis's unprotected jaw, resulting in a knockout. Rahman became the new heavyweight champion.

In Rahman's first title defense, he fought a rematch with Lennox Lewis on November 17, 2001. Rahman lost the first three rounds, being totally beaten by Lewis, in the rematch. This time in round four, Lewis scores a one-punch, right-hook knockout to win back his title.

Rahman had a big fight, after the Lewis loss, on June 1, 2002, against Evander Holyfield for the WBA elimination. In the Holyfield match, Rahman lost by a technical decision after being headbutted by Holyfield that caused a massive swelling on Rahman's forehead.

Rahman would fight two top contenders in 2003, but he was out of shape. He first fought David Tua on March 29, 2003, for the IBF elimination fight. Rahman knocked Tua down, and everyone thought that he had won by a decision, but the judges called it a draw. He lost to John Ruiz on December 13, 2003.

Rahman's first four fights of 2004 were against not-too-tough fighters, winning in all of them. These four wins would set him up with a fight with Kali Meehan on November 13, 2007. This would be a number one contender fight to the title. Rahman won by a fourth-round knockout over Meehan.

With the win over Kali Meehan, Rahman earned a title fight with Vitali Klitschko for the *Ring Magazine* belt, which is one of the titles I believe in, and for the WBC belt. The Vitali Klitschko and Rahman fight would be postponed three times because of injury to Klitschko. In the meantime Rahman fought and beat Monte Barnet on August 13, 2005, to win the WBC Interim heavyweight championship. Vitali Klitschko would later retire in November of 2005, and the WBC named Rahman as the new world heavyweight champion.

Rahman defended the WBC title against James Toney on March 18, 2006, that ended in a draw. On his next defense of the WBC title, he fought Oleg Maskaer on August 12, 2006, and lost his title to Maskaer by a twelve-round decision.

Rahman continued to fight through 2007 and got a title shot with the champion, Wladimir Klitschko, on December 13, 2008. Rahman lost his title shot with Klitschko, getting knocked out in the seventh round. Before this fight, Wladimir Klitschko had won the unification fight to be the world champion ten months earlier.

Vitali Klitschko

Johnson fields a right from Klitschko.

Crying is okay, but cursing is not.

Klitschko has Arreola in trouble.

Vitali Klitschko congratulates his brother Wladimir immediately after Wladimir stopped Ruslan Chagaev to win the *Ring* heavyweight championship in June 2009. Richard Schaefer, CEO of Golden Boy Promotions, relieves a match between Haye, and one of the Klistchkos could generate as much as $120 million.

Vitali Klitschko

Born: 1971, Ukraine
Weight: 247 lb., 6'7"
Champion: 2004-2005

Won: 39   Lost: 2   Drew: 0   Knockouts: 37

Vitali Klitschko was a fighter with skills, punching power; strong, superior reach; and a consistent puncher. He also was a very educated fighter; he has a PhD in sports science from the University of Kiev in 2000.

Before boxing, Vitali was very good at kickboxing. In November of 1993 he took part in the World Amateur Championship of WAKO, held in Atlantic City, New Jersey. He made it all the way to the final match, where he got defeated by Pele Reid. As a professional kickboxer, Vitali won the super heavyweight championship at the first World Military Games in Italy in 1995. 1995 was a busy year for Vitali as he also won silver medal at the 1995 World Amateur Boxing Championship in Berlin Germany, where he was defeated by Russia's Alexei Lezin in the finals.

In 1996 Vitali turned professional and had his first professional fight on November 16, 1996, knocking out Tony Bradham in two rounds. Winning all his fights in 1997, Vitali would win two titles in 1998. He won the WBO Intercontinental title with a fifth-round knockout over Dick Ryan on May 2, 1998. Then on October 24, 1998, he won the European heavyweight title with a second-round knockout over Germany's Mario Schiesser.

The year 1999 would bring Vitali the WBO world title. He had twenty-four fights, winning all of them either by knockout or TKO, with his fights being short. On Vitali's twenty-fifth fight, he fought Herbie Hide for the WBO heavyweight title on June 26,

1999. The fight lasted just two rounds, with Vitali winning by a knockout to be the WBO champion.

Vital defended his title two times before the year was up in 1999, winning both of them by knockout and by TKO. On Vitali's third defense of his title, he fought a contender named Chris Byrd on April 1, 2000. In the fight, Vitali was winning big on all three judges' scorecards. Then he tore his left rotator cuff that had him in so much pain he had to quit in the ninth round. Because of this, many boxing fans looked at him as being a soft fighter, and he lost his WBO title.

After the loss to Chris Byrd, Vitali would win five straight fights from April of 2000 to November of 2002. He also won the WBA Intercontinental title by beating Orlin Norris by a knockout in the first round on January 27, 2001. These wins earn him a title fight with the champion Lennox Lewis.

Lennox Lewis and Vitali fought on June 21, 2003. Going into the fight, Vitali was a 4-1 underdog. He dominated Lewis the first two rounds, landing hard rights and stunning Lewis in the second round by two hard rights. In the third and fourth round, Lewis landed some big rights that open up two major gashes over and under Vitali's left eye. As the fight went on, the cuts got worse. After the six rounds, the ring doctor stopped the fight, even though Vitali wanted to continue to fight. Lewis won by a TKO because it was by a punch and not by a headbutt. At the end of fight, Vitali was leading on all three judges' cards: 58-56.

When he lost the WBO title to Chris Byrd in 2000 by throwing in the towel because of an injured shoulder, he was criticized for quitting in the fight. Now with his great showing against Lennox Lewis and leading in points at the end of the fight, he gained world respect for his great showing against the heavyweight champion. A rematch was planned right away, but Lewis retired from the ring six months after their fight. Vitali then defeated Kirk Johnson by a two-round knockout.

With Lennox Lewis now retired, the *Ring Magazine* recognized the winner of the fight between Vitali Klitschko and Corrie Sanders to be the world champion. Corrie Sanders had knocked out Wladimir Klitschko in two rounds in 2003 for the WBO title. Vitali and Sanders were the top two fighters when the title was vacant by Lewis's retirement. Vitali and Corrie Sanders fought for the title on April 24, 2004. In the fight, Vitali gave Sanders a serious beating in the eighth round until the referee stopped it. Since Lennox Lewis retired, the *Ring Magazine* had a new champion.

After the Sanders fight came the only defense of his title against Danny Williams on December 11, 2004. Williams had just knocked out Mike Tyson in four rounds on July 30, 2004. In the fight against Vitali, Williams was overmatched, bloodied, and battered. Vitali knocked Williams down four times and gave him a savage beating until the referee finally stopped it in the eighth round. Vitali dominated by outpunching him, 296-44. He would say that it was the best he had fought in his career.

A string of injuries that would have him out of the ring leading to his retirement from the ring came after the Williams fight. The recent injury was a knee injury that he suffered while in training for a fight with Hasim Rahman, which had been postponed for the fourth time because of Vitali's injuries.

Vitali retired from the ring on November 9, 2005, because of mounting injuries. While he was retired from boxing, he ran for mayor of Kiev in 2006 and lost but was elected to the Kiev City Council. In 2008 he was appointed to the Ukrainian delegation of the Congress of the Council of Europe.

After being retired from the ring since 2005, Vitali made a comeback to the ring on October 11, 2008, against Samuel Peteri. The WBC said that this would be a title fight. Vitali gave Peteri a sound beating that Peteri retired on his stool at the end of the eighth round. He was now the WBC champion. Vitali successfully defended his title three times, winning all of them. His last win since I wrote this was against Kevin Johnson on December of 2009. He has not retired and is still the WBC champion as I am writing this on January of 2010. With the total fights he has in his career, Vitali has the best knockouts percentage, at 94.9 percent, than any heavyweight champion in history.

Wladimir Klitschko

Is Wladimir a lock to keep the Ring belt another year?　　　Wiadimir and Panettiere (far left) pose with philanthropist Diana Jenkins.

One of the challengers on Lewis's agenda is Wladimir Klitschko, pictured defeating Jameel McCline. Former heavyweight champ George Foreman thinks the young, strong, talented Klitschko might have what it takes to bump off the thirty-seven-year-old Lewis.

Ray Austin folded inside two rounds.

Wladimir Klitschko

Born: 1976, Ukraine
Weight: 242 lbs, 6'6"
Champion: 2009-Present

Won: 53   Lost: 3   Drew: 0   Knockouts: 47

Wladimir Klitschko was a very smart fighter who runs the rounds the way he wants it to go; he has knockout power and a strong jab. Like his brother Vitali, he also was a very educated fighter, having gone to Kiev University where he got a PhD in 2001. He also speaks four languages: English, Russian, Ukrainian, and German.

He got interested in boxing at the age of fourteen and was fighting as an amateur in 1993. Wladimir won the Junior European Championship as a heavyweight. In 1994 he came in second place at the Junior World Championship in Turkey. In the 1995 Military Championship in Italy, he won the gold medal. In 1996 he came in second place as a super heavyweight at the European Championship in Denmark. Wladimir would get a greater fame at the 1996 summer Olympics in Atlanta, Georgia, where he won the super heavyweight gold medal.

Wladimir turned professional in 1996. He had his first professional fight on November 16, 1996, fighting and beating Fabian Meza by a first-round knockout. He would go on and have a 16-0 record, with all early-round knockouts except for one. On February 15, 1997, he fought Charles Monroe. In the fight, Wladimir was winning when Monroe was disqualified in the sixth round for headbutting.

On Wladimir's seventh fight, he fought and beat by a third-round knockout Marcus McIntyre on February 14, 1998, for the vacant WBC international heavyweight title.

In a rematch with Carlos Monroe, Wladimir knocked out Monroe with a one-punch right in the sixth round on August 6, 1998.

Wladimir had a record of 24-0 with twenty-one knockouts when he fought Ross Puritty for his twenty-fifth fight on December 5, 1998. Ross Puritty was a journeyman fighter, with a record of 24-13-1. The fight with Puritty, Wladimir suffered his first loss in a big upset and lost his WBC international heavyweight title. In the fight, by the tenth round, Wladimir was exhausted. In the eleventh round, Puritty pounded Wladimir until his trainer stopped the fight.

After suffering his first professional loss to end the year 1998, Wladimir would win seven straight fights in 1999, including two titles. On July 17, 1999, he fought and beat Joseph Chingangu by a fifth-round knockout to win the vacant WBA Inter-Continental heavyweight title. On his next fight, he fought and beat Axel Schulz by an eighth-round knockout on September 25, 1999, to win the EBU (European) heavyweight title.

After having a good year in 1999, Wladimir had another good year in 2000. He had four fights, winning all of them, and won two more titles. Wladimir fought and beat Paea Wofgramm by a first-round knockout for the vacant WBC international heavyweight title on March 18, 2000. Wladimir fought Chris Byrd for the WBO title on October 14, 2000. In the fight, Wladimir knocked down Byrd in the ninth and eleventh round to win the WBO title by a unanimous decision.

The year 2001 and 2002 bought Wladimir five more fights and five more knockouts; one of his wins was a fight with a top contender in Ray Mercer on June 29, 2002. In the fight Wladimir knocked Mercer down in the first round by two left hooks. The referee stopped the fight in the sixth round when Mercer was being hit by a lot of punches and not answering them.

With a record of 40-1, Wladimir had his second loss on March 8, 2003, against Corrie Sanders. In the fight Sanders knocked Wladimir down two times in the first round and twice in the second, getting knocked out in the second round. This was the biggest upset of the year 2003. After the loss to Sanders, Wladimir would close out the year 2003 with two knockout wins.

Wladimir started 2004 year like he started 2003, with a loss. On April 10, 2004, he fought Lamon Brewster for the vacant WBO heavyweight title. In the fourth round, Wladimir knocked Brewster down; then in the fifth round, Brewster knocked Wladimir down. He would get up to beat the count and fell back to the canvas, and the referee stopped it.

The loss to Lamon Brewster would be his last loss leading up to winning the *Ring Magazine* heavyweight title and to be included into my book of champions. To get to that, he had to win all his fights and collect some titles along the way.

After the Brewster loss, Wladimir won three fights in a row. His fourth fight was against Chris Byrd for the IBF title on April 22, 2006. In the fight Byrd was knocked down twice by hard rights in the fifth and seventh round, and had Byrd bleeding from a cut. The referee stopped the fight in the seventh round, and Wladimir had the IBF title.

Wladimir won his next two fights by knockouts over Calvin Brock and Ray Austin. On his next fight, Wladimir got the chance to avenge his loss against Lamon Brewster on July 7, 2007. Although he fought most of the fight with a broken middle left finger in his left hand, he was able to stop Brewster in six rounds.

Next fight for Wladimir was with the WBO champion Sultan Ibragimov on February 23, 2008. Wladimir won the fight by a unanimous decision.

Wladimir's next two fights were knockouts over Tony Thompson and Hasim Rahman. Then came the big fight with the WBA champion Rusian Chagaer; this fight would be for Wladimir IBF, WBO, IBO world titles; and for Chagaer WBA title. This fight would also be for the *Ring Magazine* heavyweight title. The fight happened on June 20, 2009. In the fight, Wladimir knocked Chagaer down in the second round. In the seventh round, Chagaer was bleeding, and he took a beating at the end of the ninth round. The ringside doctor stopped the fight at the end of the ninth round. Wladimir became the first *Ring Magazine* champion since his brother Vitali retired in 2005.

As I have stopped writing this book in 2010, Wladimir Klitschko is still the world heavyweight champion with a record of 52-3.

Promoters of the Century

Tex Rickard

Born: 1870-1929
Kansas City, Missouri
Promoter: 1900s-1920s

George (Tex) Rickard

Rickard owned his own gambling saloon when he started promoting fights. He promoted the classic fight that everybody in the country wanted in champion Jack Johnson versus former undefeated retired champion Jim Jefferies in 1910. He also set the promotion record with champion Jess Willard vs. Frank Moran in 1916 with a gate of $156,000.

Rickard had a meal ticket in champion Jack Dempsey. He promoted boxing's first million-dollar gate with Dempsey vs. Georges Carpenter in 1921. With Dempsey as champion, Rickard went on and had five straight million-dollar gate fights. Rickard promoted the rematch between champion Gene Tunney vs. Dempsey that was the first two-million-dollar gate fight. Like famous promoters who would come after him, Rickard had his share of legal difficulties with other promoters and financiers.

Rickard was great for boxing because he took boxing to another level, with new audiences and public interest.

Mike Jacobs

Born: 1880-1953
New York
Promoter: 1930s-1940s

Jacobs (right) with Joe Louis (left) and Louis' trainer Jack "Chappie" Blackburn ringside at the Henry Armstrong/Barney Ross bout at the Madison Square Garden Bowl, Long Island City, Queens, New York on May 31, 1938

Jacobs worked under Tex Rickard in promoting in the 1910s. Like Rickard had Dempsey, Jacobs had a gold mine in Joe Louis. Before Louis became champion, Jacobs had a million-dollar gate fight between Louis vs. Max Baer in 1935. Joe Louis was champion from 1937-1949, and Jacobs promoted all of Louis's twenty-five title defenses. Jacobs had three-million-dollar gate fights. At one time he promoted all of the champions in all of the different weight divisions.

Donald (Don) King

Born: 1931
Cleveland, Ohio
Promoter: 1970s-2000s

King started making money by running an illegal bookmaking operation. He was one of the top number bankers in Cleveland. He was in the numbers business for years, making big money. With the right connections, he became a big hit as a promoter. King was great with reporters; going in details, story- telling and being very flamboyant.

In the '70s, King had the premier heavyweight fights. He promoted the Muhammed Ali vs. George Foreman Rumble in the Jungle. He also promoted the Ali vs. Joe Frazier: The Thrilla in Manila.

In the '70s he also had an impressive list of fighters, like Larry Holmes, Wilfred Benitez, Roberto Duran, and Alexis Arguello.

By the '80s and '90s, he was promoting all the top fighters, among them Mike Tyson, Evander Holyfield, Julio Cesar Chavez, Aaron Pryor, Bernard Hopkins, Felix Trinidad, Mike McCallum, Meldrick Taylor, and many more.

King wore his hair in an electric style. He could mesmerize and overwhelm you. He could talk you into anything. Fighters and managers came to King because they knew that he could make money for everyone. King was constantly in court because of lawsuits concerning money

Robert (Bob) Arum

Born: 1931
New York
Promoter: 1970s-2000s

Arum was a very educated man, having gone to New York University and Harvard Law School. He used his education to work for him as a promoter.

He had promoted a lot of super fights, like Marvin Hagler vs. Roberto Duran, Hagler vs. John Mugabi, Sugar Ray Leonard vs. Hagler, Evander Holyfield vs. George Foreman, and a lot of other super fights.

Arum also had his own fighters in Oscar De La Hoya and Manny Pacquiao. He was also a big rival to Don King. As a promoter, Arum was involved in many controversies. He is the founder and CEO of Top Rank, a professional boxing promotion company in Las Vegas, NV.

Facts About the
Heavyweight Division

First Championship Fight on Film:

March 17, 1989 — Robert Fitzsimmons
Knockout Champion — James Corbett in 14 rounds

First Championship Fight on Radio Broadcast:

July 2, 1921 — Jack Dempsey
Knocked out George Carpentier in four rounds

First Championship Televised:

December 5, 1947 — Joe Louis won a decision over Jersey Joe
Walcott.

Champion Who Has Won Title Two Times:

Floyd Patterson — 1956, 1960
Muhammad Ali — 1964, 1974
George Foreman — 1973, 1994
Evander Holyfield — 1990, 1993
Lennox Lewis — 1999, 2001

Champion Who Has Won Title Three Times:

Muhammad Ali — 1964, 1974, 1978

The Biggest Age Spread of Any Championship Fight:

Nineteen years, George Foreman vs. Michael Moorer

Other Than an American to Win the Title:

Robert Fitzsimmons—England, 1897-1899
Tommy Burns—Canada, 1906-1908
Max Schmeling—Germany, 1930-1932
Primo Carnera—Italy, 1933-1934
Ingemar Johansson—Sweden, 1959-1960
Lennox Lewis—England, 1999-2001 and 2001-2004
Vitali Klitschko—Ukraine, 2004-2005
Wladimir Klitschko—Ukraine, 2009-Present

Most Fights After Losing the Title:

Ezzard Charles—43, 1951-1959

Most Time Defending the Title:

Joe Louis—25, 1937-1949

Champions Who Never Lost While Champion:

James Jeffries, 1899-1904
Gene Tunney, 1926-1928
Joe Louis, 1937-1949
Rocky Marciano, 1952-1956
Vitali Klitschko, 2004-2005

Champions Who Won Gold Medal Olympics:

Middleweight—Floyd Patterson in 1952 and Michael Spinks in 1976

Light Heavyweight—Muhammad Ali (Cassius Clay) 1960 and
    Leon Spinks 1976
Heavyweight—Joe Frazier 1964, George Foreman 1968, Lennox
    Lewis 1988,
Wladimir Klitschko 1996

Champion Who Won Titles in Different Divisions:

Robert Fitzsimmons—Middleweight 1891, Heavyweight 1897,
    Light Heavyweight 1903
Gene Tunney—Light Heavyweight 1922, Heavyweight 1926
Michael Spinks—Light Heavyweight 1981, Heavyweight 1985
Evander Holyfield—Cruiserweight 1986, Heavyweight 1990 and
    1993
Michael Moore—Light Heavyweight 1988, Heavyweight 1994

Longest Years as Champion:

Joe Louis, 11 years and 9 months

Longest Title Fight:

John L. Sullivan knocked out Jaka Kilrain in round 75

Tallest Champion:

Vitali Klitschko—6'7"

Heaviest Champion:

Primo Carnera—260 1/2 pounds

Longest Reach:

Primo Carnera—85 1/2 inches

Relatives to Win a Title:

Leon and Michael Spinks — Brothers
Vitali and Wladimir Klitschko — Brothers

Most Knockdowns in a Title Fight:

Joe Louis, 22

Light Heavyweight to Win a Heavyweight Title:

Michael Spinks
Michael Moorer

Southpaw to Be Champion:

Michael Moorer

Most Knockdowns in a Round (7):

Jack Dempsey vs. Jess Willard 1919
Ingemar Johansson vs. Floyd Patterson 1959
Jack Dempsey vs. Luis Firpo 1923

Longest time to Be Champion a Second Time:

George Foreman — 20 years

Shortest Amount of Fights to Become World Champion:

Leon Spinks, 7

Biggest Odds on Fight to Win:

Mike Tyson was a 42-1 favorite to beat Buster Douglas

Biggest Fist:

Sonny Listen—15 inches

Oldest Champion to Win Title:

George Foreman—45

Youngest to Win Championship:

Mike Tyson—21 years and 32 days

Most Fights in a Career:

Ezzard Charles—1940-1959 with 122 matches

Undefeated in Total Career:

Rocky Marciano—1947-1956 with 49-0

Most First-Round Knockout's:

Jack Dempsey with 24

"As a champion, you must do and don't do the following"

A. Stay a Busy Fighter

A lot of the greatest champions of all time lost their titles by not staying busy. By not staying busy, you lose the edge that you had to get you to where you were as the champion. Your reflexes would decline; you may not be at your regular weight and would be older or feel to have gotten older faster.

John L. Sullivan was out of the ring for three years when he defended his title against Jim Corbett. By this time in the fight with Corbett, Sullivan had lost his edge. His reflexes were bad, his weight was over twenty pounds than normal, and he had aged. He lost his title badly to Corbett by a knockout. In Sullivan's last fight, three years before he had gone seventy-five rounds in beating Jake Kilmin.

Jack Dempsey was out of the ring for three years when he defended his title against Gene Tunney. By this time in the fight with Tunney, Dempsey had lost his edge. His reflexes were off, and he had aged quickly as a fighter. He lost his title easily to Tunney. Dempsey's last fight three years before had been won in a two-round knockout over Luis Firpo.

Jess Willard was out of the ring for three years when he defended his title against Jack Dempsey. By this time in the fight with Dempsey, Willard had lost his edge; also his reflexes were bad, and he had aged quickly as a fighter. He lost his title to Dempsey in four rounds. In Willard's last fight, three years before he had won a decision over Frank Moran.

B. Don't Underestimate Your Opponent

Some fighters had lost their title because they were sure that they were going to win, didn't take their opponent serious, didn't train as hard as they should, and just didn't go about the fight right.

Max Baer was a 10-1 favorite to beat James Braddock in his defense of his title fight in 1935. Baer, who went along with the odds favoring him to keep his title, was quoted as saying, "I'll keep the title for at least five years and then I'll retire like Tunney did, and live like a king."

Baer didn't take the fight seriously and said that he would knock Braddock out inside of six rounds. He also didn't train properly for this fight; Baer fought listlessly for most of the fight. He was in poor condition, was tied by the eight round, and his punches didn't have the normal power in them.

Baer lost the fight and his title to Jim Braddock by a unanimous decision. In his last fight, in which he had won the title from Primo Carnera, he had won by a knockout in the eleventh round.

Muhammed Ali was a very big favorite to beat Leon Spinks in his defense of his title in 1978. Ali took Spink very lightly because Spinks had only seven professional fights, and he was unranked in the top ten contenders to the title. Ali didn't really want the fight at first because of the few fights that Spinks had. No champion had ever won a championship with such few fights. For this fight Ali didn't train right, didn't eat right, didn't spar enough rounds, didn't work out in the gym, and just didn't take Spinks seriously.

By not training right for the fight, Ali got tired in the late rounds. Spinks trained very hard for this fight and was scoring in the late rounds. He was psyched and punched nonstop throughout the fight. Ali lost to Leon Spinks by a decision and also lost his title. In the rematch with Spinks, Ali trained hard and won back his title by a decision.

C. Don't Be an Old Fighter

This can go either way to go on and fight late in your career or quit fighting because of old age. There are a lot of reasons why fighters fight late, well past their prime years. This can be for the need of money, thinking he still has it to win or maybe just for the fame. For all of these reasons, it usually comes out bad for the fighters who want to fight late in their career. They are now fighting younger and hungrier fighters that they once were, but no longer are because they already had it and can't ever get it back.

Jim Jefferies was champion from 1899 to 1905 when he decided to retire from the ring as the undefeated world champion. He was twenty-nine years old. Jefferies was talked into coming out of retirement to become the great white hope to beat the black champion Jack Johnson in 1910. Jefferies for this fight was thirty-five years old and Johnson was twenty-six years old. Jefferies was way past his prime and was beaten easily by a TKO in fifteen rounds. This fight with Johnson would be the only fight that Jefferies lost and the only fight that he was knocked off his feet. The last fight that Jefferies had before Johnson was in 1904 when he knocked out Jack Monroe in two rounds.

Joe Louis was the champion from 1937 to 1949 when he decided to retire as the undefeated world champion. Louis was having serious money problems with his taxes and needed money badly. He made a comeback to the ring in 1950.

Ezzard Charles was the current champion in 1950, and Louis was thirty-six years old. Louis was way past his prime in this fight and was just a shadow of the real Joe Louis. Louis's reflexes were rusty, he wasn't fast, and he got cut up. Ezzard Charles kept his title by beating Louis easily in a fifteen-round decision. Joe Louis's last fight before Charles was in 1948 when he knocked out Jersey Joe Walcott in eleven rounds.

Muhammad Ali was champion the third time from 1978 to 1978 when he decided to retire as the undefeated champion of the world. Ali was already the only champion to win the title three times, had the hunger of the ring, and thought that he could win back the title a fourth time.

After being retired for two years, Ali made a comeback to fight the current champion Larry Holmes in 1980. Ali was now thirty-eight years old. In the fight it was a big mismatch as Holmes won every round easily. Holmes, because of respect to Ali, even held back his punches because he didn't want to inflict worse pain to Ali. Finally in the eleventh round, Ali's manager stopped the mismatch fight to save Ali. This would be the first time in Ali's sixty-one-fight career that he had been

KOed. Ali's last fight before Holmes was against Leon Spinks in 1978 when he beat Spinks for the title.

D. Know When to Retire and Stay Retired

Two of boxing greatest champions knew when to retire and stayed retired. This is hard to do, especially when you are still young, still real good, and the contenders at the time are not that good.

Jim Jeffries, Joe Louis, and Muhammed Ali all knew when to retire. They retired because of their age, not having worthy opponents, having enough money, or just not having the hunger for the ring anymore. All three, Jeffries, Louis, and Ali, knew when to retire; and they were right. All three also made the mistake of coming back to the ring and not staying retired.

Gene Tunney was a great champion from 1926 until he retired from the ring in 1928. When Tunney retired as champion, he didn't really have to. He was only thirty years old and probably in the prime of his boxing career. He was an unmarked fighter, and no fighter at the time could beat him.

With his two wins over Jack Dempsey (that was boxing all-time records, million-dollar gate fights), Tunney had all the money that he ever needed saved up. Unlike a lot of other fighters who go broke, Tunney spent his money wisely. Tunney never made a comeback to the ring, although the promoters over the years tried to get him back, but he wouldn't. Tunney became a successful millionaire businessman instead.

Rocky Marciano was a great champion from 1952 until he retired from the ring in 1956. He was thirty-three years old, still strong, and in excellent condition. The contenders that were there at the time could not beat him.

Marciano knew in his last two fights that Ezzard Charles had damaged his nose. Archie Moore had knocked him down, and training for a fight would be harder for him. He also had been pressured by his wife to retire to spend more time with the family. He had made enough money from boxing to live comfortably. Marciano would say that if Joe Louis could not make a successful comeback, he wouldn't try. He became the only heavyweight champion in history to be undefeated in all of his fights, at 49-0, by not making a comeback.

Challengers—Some Things to Know to Win

As a challenger to the champion, I would suggest that you must do the following:

A. Always be the aggressor.
B. Be smarter on the offensive and defensive ends of the fight.
C. Set the pace for yourself early in the fight so that it will work for you in the latter rounds.
D. Work harder.
E. Allow the champion to be overconfident of the victory, but not you the challenger. A lot of championships were lost in this book because of overconfidence.
F. Always have something positive going on in your head in every round. If there is not much action going on, the round will be given to the champion.
G. Always train hard to go the distance if you need to.

The champion has his title, and it is the task of the challenger to take it from him.

The Best Career of All the Champions

All of the heavyweight champions had a great career in boxing. To go from wanting to be a boxer, to an amateur career, to your first professional fight, all the way up to be the world heavyweight champion is a great career. I picked out four champions who I thought had the best career.

A. Jack Johnson

I thought that Johnson had to go through so much to be the champion and to get the chance to be a champion. He was ready to fight for the title as early as before Jim Jeffries retired in 1905. Even when Tommy Burns was the champion, Johnson had to run him down from country to country and keep it in the paper to get a title shot. When you are the first black to challenge for the title and to be the champion, it is always going to be hard.

As a black heavyweight champion, Johnson was the most hated black man in the world. He had gone through a lot in the seven years that he was champion. Today a manager will look for a fighter to beat a champion. When Johnson was champion, the whole country was looking for a great white hope. For years he would beat their white hope and taunt their fighter, even in a crowd of all whites with anyone of them could have guns. To do this and marry three white women in the early 1900s tells me that he had heart, more than I would have had at that time. Remember this was forty years before Jackie Robinson broke in as the first black baseball player, and he had big problems doing that. With all the pressure that Johnson had on him, he is still regarded as one of the greatest champions ever.

B. Joe Louis

To me, Joe Louis's being the world heavyweight champion for almost twelve years is unheard of. This is hard to do for a lot of different reasons. To be champion for almost twelve years means you were beating fighters when you were young, getting old, and beating fighters when you were old as a fighter.

Being champion for so many years means having a lot of title defenses, even as he was getting older; Louis had a total of twenty-five defenses of his titles against the top fighters, ducking no contender and fighting often. Out of the twenty-five times that he defended his titles, he only went the distance three times, and the other twenty two-were by knockouts with seven of the knockouts in the first round. With Joe Louis's record of years as champion and twenty-five defenses of his title, I can't see any of these two records ever being broken.

C. Rocky Marciano

To go undefeated a whole professional boxing career is almost unheard of. To be 49-0 with that many fights from the start when you haven't reached your peak to your championship years is hard to do. To fight all the top contenders at the time you are champion, clean up the division, and still retire undefeated is hard to do. This is special because out of all the heavyweight champions from 1882 through 2010, it has happened only once, and the one fighter is Rocky Marciano.

D. Muhammad Ali

Muhammad Ali's career is much different from the career of Jack Johnson, Joe Louis, and Rocky Marciano. Johnson Louis's and Marciano's career continue on, with Louis making a comeback that I am not even counting that part in Louis career.

Ali was champion from 1964 to 1967. At the time he was stripped of his title, no man on earth could beat him, hardly any fighter could hit him, and he was compared to all of the all time greats in the heavyweight division. Most of all, he was only twenty-five years old.

To be stripped of your title and banned from boxing for three years and come back to be world champion two more times is unbelievable. He was not only the champion but the undisputed world champion. To me, the reason why I say this is unbelievable is that the world probably never saw the best of Ali after they took his title in 1967 when he was twenty-five years old. When they said he could fight again, he was twenty-eight.

To me Ali was unbeatable when he was champion from 1964-1967. At the time he was twenty-two to twenty-five-years old. I believe seriously that the years they took his title and banned him from 1967-1970 would have been his prime years. Ali would have been twenty-five to twenty-eight years old; he would have still been young and a better, smarter fighter. Those are the years that the world did not see — Ali in his prime.

Instead the world saw the Ali being out of the ring for three years, not at his best, slower on foot movement, slower on hand speed, and starting over at twenty-eight years of age. With all this happening to him, Muhammad Ali was still able to make a comeback to the ring after a three-year layoff to win the world heavyweight title two more times. At this stage of his career, he had ring smarts.

The Best Comeback Champion Ever: George Foreman

Percentage wise, it's not good for a fighter to make a comeback to the ring after their career in the ring is over. A lot of former fighters and former champions had tried; and in the ring they looked very bad, old, embarrassing, taking a very lopsided beating.

To me only two former champions had ever done good coming back to the ring. Muhammad Ali did well after three years out of the ring. George Foreman to me is tops because he was out of the ring so long. He was out of the ring for ten years, which is seven big years more than Ali. When Foreman came back to the ring, he was forty years old, compared to Ali being twenty-eight years old when he returned to the ring—a big twelve-year difference.

George Foreman started his boxing career in 1969 at the age of twenty. He retired from the ring in 1977 at the age of twenty-eight. At this age most champions are still fighting in their form, or even still champion.

Most former champions who made comebacks to the ring, made the mistake of coming back, knowing that they are old and don't have much time left. They want the big fights or the championship fight right now with these fast big fighters right away and they get beat badly and they look bad.

Foreman had a different plan than the other fighters. Like the other fighters, Foreman knew that he was too old; at forty he was older than the other fighters who came back. He went the opposite way in picking his opponent to fight. He didn't want the tough fights or the championship fight at the time he made his comeback. Foreman was in no hurry to embarrass himself. He wanted the easy fights first, working his way to the top and also getting himself in shape. At the time he made his comeback, he was weighing almost 270 pounds.

By having a great plan, he won twenty-four out of twenty-four of his fights. Foreman was forty-two years old and earned a chance to fight Evander Holyfield for the title in 1991, which he lost by a decision to Holyfield.

Before he fought Holyfield, people didn't take him seriously. Foreman was now older, slower, and about fifty pounds overweight. He had fought only one ranked opponent in Adilson Rodriquez. People began to take him seriously as he continued to win.

Still fighting and doing well with a 27-2 record, Foreman fought the new champion Michael Moorer for the title in 1994 at the age of forty-five years old. This time fighting for the title for the second time in his comeback, he won the championship by knocking Moorer out in the tenth round to become the oldest fighter to win the title at forty-five.

Not only did I pick Foreman because he won the title back at such an old age, but also because of the big money he made by his comeback to the ring. His comeback in the ring, he made over twenty-seven million.

Because Foreman was so much popular the second time around than he was the first time around, he made huge money in endorsements. His big endorsement was with Meineke Mufflers, and the biggest being the partnership of George Foreman Grill. Foreman would make over two hundred million in endorsement, more than he made as a fighter. He never would have made all this money in the ring and his endorsement had he not made a comeback to the ring.

With the winning of the heavyweight title, the millions he made in the ring, and the millions he made in endorsements he received, it was more than worth the comeback to the ring. This I think is Foreman's biggest accomplishment and by far the best champion to make a comeback.